THE MOVIE BUFF'S BOOK 2

Edited by

TED SENNETT

Pyramid Books **New York**

ACKNOWLEDGMENTS

Once again I should like to thank all the writers who contributed to this book for their expertise and their cooperation. And a very special note of gratitude to Jerry Vermilye for looking over all the material with the practiced eye of a movie "maven," and to Curtis Brown, who again checked all the quizzes with his unbeatable patience, good humor, and skill.

For my wife Roxane, and my children Bob, David, and Karen, my thanks for their support, and for proving that sometimes, families are even more fun than the movies.

Photographs: Jerry Vermilye, The Memory Shop, Gene Andrewski, Movie Star News, Cinemabilia, and Columbia Pictures.

CONTENTS

INTRODUCTION

By Ted Sennett

What does a movie buff mean when he says he "loves" the movies?

Many critics and film scholars have tried to define that love. Most movie buffs simply experience it: in a scene of exhilarating beauty, or a moment of explosive laughter, or, on rare occasions, an entire film that enriches their lives.

This love, of course, takes many forms. From Johnny Weissmuller to Lina Wertmuller, from the Marx Brothers to the Maysles Brothers, movie buffs will always respond differently to the ideas, moods, and images projected on the screen. Bring together a group of enthusiastic movie-lovers, and you may decide that there are as many kinds of buffs as there are movies.

In the first *Movie Buff's Book*, we presented a wide range of materials designed to entertain, inform, and challenge *all* kinds of movie buffs. The response was gratifying, and we are now pleased to present a second volume, with an entirely new collection of articles by writers devoted to the study of film, quizzes that should keep your movie memory working overtime, and photographs of your favorite players and movies.

In this book, as in the first, the guiding principle is the love of movies. And, as Errol Flynn might have said to Olivia de Havilland, such love cannot be denied.

ONE:
"LET'S TALK ABOUT MOVIES"

Place any two movie buffs in a room together and in no time at all, they're probably arguing about the merits of a particular film, reminiscing about their favorite musical or Western, or just happily comparing notes on their movie-going experiences.

We're doing the same in this first section: discussing—and challenging your memories of—many of your best-loved movies and types of movies. We also have the photographs to stir those memories.

We begin with an article on someone whom most movie buffs regard with a mixture of exasperation and affection: that mythical movie gentleman known as Oscar. . . .

NOBODY'S FAVORITE UNCLE

By Jeanine Basinger

According to Bette Davis, he was epicene, but his back-view was exactly the same as that of her first husband, Harmon Oscar Nelson. Thus, she dubbed the first of her two Academy of Motion Picture Arts and Sciences statuettes with the name of "Oscar"... and said the world picked up on the joke. Sidney Skolsky said nothing about his mate's backside, but he did claim in his syndicated gossip column that *he* was the originator of the nickname. The Academy itself stated definitely that its executive director, Mrs. Margaret Herrick, was the official author of the informal title. "Why, he looks just like my Uncle Oscar," she is said to have observed, when she first spotted a copy of the statuette on an executive's desk, way back in 1931. Presumably no one ever asked Mrs. Herrick to elaborate on this bald and naked uncle, with the flat head, peculiar eyes, and shiny skin. We are left to assume that either he worked as a chandelier holder in the Ziegfeld Follies or as an usher at Radio City Music Hall. (The logical question to have asked Mrs. Herrick was "Are there any more at home like him?")

Whoever named the award—and there is no reason to doubt Mrs. Herrick's story—remains a less interesting fact than the award itself. "Oscar" not only became the most familiar show business nickname in the world, but also sired a long line of similar awards: Tony, Emmy, Patsy, and Grammy, among others. Despite his cozy familial title, however, Oscar is nobody's favorite uncle.

Like an annual Rite of Spring, the Oscarcast (the television broadcast of the presentation) takes place among predictions (usually wrong), critical pans of the show itself (usually right), and the bestowing of the awards themselves (usually some right ones and some wrong ones). As soon as the show is over, public criticism descends not only on the winners, but also on the presenters, the Academy president's opening speech, the entertainment, the commercials in-between announcements, and even the clothes the participants wear. It's reviled as vulgar and tasteless. It's damned as boring and commercial. It's the Who Cares Event of the Year. Whoever's relative he is, Oscar is the uncle they love to hate.

Except, of course, that everyone even remotely connected with films wants him for a permanent house guest. And everyone who is even remotely a film fan faithfully watches the award presentations every year. Scrutiny of the history of the awards reveals Uncle Oscar to be a capricious fellow, unpredictable and unruly, given to un-expected decisions, susceptible to trends, and a false lover who is even rumored to be something of a jinx. So how to woo him, how to win him—that is always the question for film people. As a lifelong follower of Oscar and his adventures, I would like to suggest the following list of rules on how to capture his heart.

1. *Make Him Feel Guilty*

When an actress who gave a great performance as Marie Antoinette in *Off With Her Head!* is overlooked in favor of a newcomer (the producer's girl friend) who played a best forgotten small part in the musical version of *Hedda Gabler* (*Hedda Get Your Gun*), she is a sure-fire bet for a future award if she can only make Oscar feel guilty.

Over the years, the apology award, based on voter guilt, has worked like a charm. For instance, Bette Davis really became a star when she played the slatternly waitress in *Of Human Bondage*. She did not, however, win Oscar for her very own. In fact, she wasn't even nominated. Instead the contenders were Grace Moore (*One Night of Love*), Norma Shearer (*The Barretts of Wimpole Street*), and Claudette Colbert (*It Happened One Night*), with Colbert the ultimate surprise winner. (She was so surprised, in fact, that she was downtown boarding a train to New York when Academy officials located her and told her she was the winner. With all the glamour of a final scene in a thirties film, Colbert dashed back to the banquet with a police escort, grabbed Oscar, posed for photographers in her traveling suit, thanked everyone in Hollywood, and flashed back to the train—all in a record seven minutes.)

The lack of a nomination for Davis kicked off one of the Academy's biggest controversies, and the following year found her cashing in on everyone's guilt. She was chosen Best Actress for her role of Joyce Heath in *Dangerous*—a role in which she proved she could act by driving a car into a tree. Even Davis admitted she shouldn't have won: "Katharine Hepburn gave by far the best performance of the year in *Alice Adams*," she said. Nevertheless, she took Uncle Oscar home anyway ... and never brought him back.

The apology award (based on the guilt technique) has also brought awards to James Stewart (who lost for his most famous role, *Mr. Smith Goes To Washington* and won the following year for a smaller part in *The Phila-*

delphia Story) and Elizabeth Taylor. Taylor's first truly mature acting job was that of the frustrated wife in *Cat on a Hot Tin Roof*, even though she had also been nominated previously for *Raintree County*. She lost both times, but two years later received her apology award for the less challenging role of a good-time girl in *Butterfield 8*. Taylor had evidently heard about Davis' case, because in *Butterfield 8* she drove a car into a highway barrier, thus suggesting a subdivision of the guilt techniques: make-him-feel-guilty-and-accept-a-role-as-a-bad-driver. (Perhaps the Academy officers merely felt that either of the two stars might drive an automobile through the front windows of the Academy if they were overlooked a second time!) At any rate, both Taylor and Davis dispensed with any gossip about deserving their Oscars by winning second ones—Davis for *Jezebel* and Taylor for *Who's Afraid of Virginia Woolf?*. Those who use the guilt method might want to be prepared to win a second time, just to make sure they deserved it the first time.

Fans usually correct award injustices for themselves. A large number of them are prepared to punch you in the nose over whether or not James Stewart won Oscar for *Mr. Smith*. Many insist that Olivia de Havilland won for *The Snake Pit*. De Havilland already had an Oscar for *To Each His Own* when she was passed over for *The Snake Pit*. She extracted a guilt Oscar from the Academy anyway, making them give her another one for *The Heiress* the next year.

Making voters feel guilty is not the prerogative of stars, of course. Directors Cecil B. DeMille and George Cukor

Spencer Tracy and Bette Davis receive their Oscars from Sir Cedric Hardwicke for the best performances of 1938, Tracy for BOYS TOWN and Davis for JEZEBEL.

have both been the benefactors of such psychology. DeMille was a Hollywood establishment figure whose sex and scandal epics defined Hollywood in many people's minds. Yet he never got within a peacock's feather of an Oscar until 1952, when one of his movies (*The Greatest Show On Earth*) was awarded an apology Oscar. DeMille himself was not named best director of the year, however. That award went to John Ford for *The Quiet Man* (Ford was a multiple winner who never had to make anyone feel guilty). Cukor finally received an award for *My Fair Lady*, after a lifetime in the business making such magnificent films as *Dinner At Eight*, *The Philadelphia Story*, *Holiday*, *Adam's Rib*, *Pat and Mike*, etc..

The greatest guilt award of all time was a double header involving Ingrid Bergman. It came about not only as a result of Bergman's having been overlooked twice (no nomination for *Casablanca* and a nomination but no win for *For Whom the Bell Tolls*), but also for the unusual circumstances of her private life. To cover the initial gaffes regarding *Casablanca* and *For Whom the Bell Tolls*, Bergman was issued an apology award for *Gaslight* (although her performance in the latter film was such a winner that fans might argue that there was no apology involved at all). Later, however, it became necessary for Oscar to cough up a second apology to Bergman. She had been socially ostracized not only by Hollywood but by the entire American public as a result of her extra-marital shenanigans with Italian director Roberto Rossellini. To welcome her home from a European exile, she was presented with an apology award for her performance in *Anastasia*. And just in case two Oscars weren't enough . . . after all, Bergman had been denounced by both Congress *and* Louella Parsons . . . she was awarded a third Oscar as best supporting actress for a minor performance in *Murder on the Orient Express*. It was murder, all right. Technically, of course, one can't murder a statuette . . . but it appears to be entirely possible to make him feel guilty!

2. *Go Out of Character*

There exists in show business a finale known as "the wow finish." It is a routine designed to jerk audiences up out of their seats and send them home thinking they saw a great show, even if they dozed off during the last half. The philosophy behind this is "if they're asleep and you wake them up, they'll think the whole show was that good but they missed it."

A stepchild to this philosophy is the "wow role." If you are a singer, go dramatic. If you are dramatic, go comic. If you are young, age fifty years, preferably in ninety minutes of running time. If you are old, look young and debonair, and kick up your heels in a fox trot . . . or parody yourself and your former roles. If you are a grande dame, dance a polka on top of a hat box, or peel a banana while standing on your head. Do something—anything—as long as Oscar doesn't expect it.

James Cagney started in show business as a dancer, but

In early 1942, Ginger Rogers presents an Oscar to Joan Fontaine for her performance the previous year in Alfred Hitchcock's SUSPICION. Rogers won a year earlier for KITTY FOYLE.

Vivien Leigh accepts her Academy Award for her performance as Scarlett O'Hara in GONE WITH THE WIND (1939).

he rarely did musical parts on film. Thus his Oscar win for singer/dancer/songwriter George M. Cohan in *Yankee Doodle Dandy* qualifies as an out-of-character "wow role." On the other hand, when dancer Ginger Rogers took off her tap shoes and played a serious role as a white collar girl in *Kitty Foyle* she won her own statuette.

Jane Wyman, usually the wisecracking confidante of the heroine, found Oscar waiting for her with open arms when she stopped with the smart remarks and played a pathetic deaf mute in *Johnny Belinda*. Humphrey Bogart, tough guy extraordinaire, found gold playing a broken-down old boat captain in *The African Queen*, while elegant and sophisticated Grace Kelly won by playing an unglamorous housewife in a shapeless sweater (*The Country Girl*).

3. Go to Broadway

The Hollywood inferiority complex is such that almost anyone who has become successful in a Broadway show has a chance at impressing Oscar. The least important chorus boy can come to California and intimidate the populace with his Big Apple credentials. And if one is a genuine Broadway name with clippings from *The New York Times* to prove it, anything goes. Consider these Broadway Intimidation Oscars:

Jose Ferrer, the jack-of-all-trades of the Great White Way (he produced, directed, and starred in plays) won for *Cyrano de Bergerac* over the more cinematic and satisfying performances of Spencer Tracy in *Father of the Bride* and William Holden in *Sunset Boulevard*.

Judy Holliday won for *Born Yesterday*, over Bette Davis and Anne Baxter in *All About Eve* and Gloria Swanson in *Sunset Boulevard*.

Shirley Booth won for *Come Back, Little Sheba*, over Joan Crawford in *Sudden Fear*, Bette Davis in *The Star*, and Susan Hayward in *With a Song In My Heart*.

The winning performances were great, too, but one can't help but feel that dear old Uncle Oscar liked to ride home with a little New York class!

4. Lie Low and Wait Until You're Old

It is a fact of show business lore that if you can stay in the game long enough, keeping on your feet until the last gasp, you eventually become known as the greatest entertainer of your type that ever existed. This entitles an actor to the "I Deserve It Because I'm Old" Oscar which can come in the form of an actual acting award or an honorary award for contributions to films over the years. After a certain point in an actor's career, it is almost axiomatic that, if he gets a nomination, he's a shoo-in for the win. John Wayne, one of Hollywood's greatest stars in terms of box-office popularity, was hardly likely to lose when nominated for *True Grit* in 1969.

Ruth Gordon won her first Oscar at the age of 72 for *Rosemary's Baby* and pointed out that awards like that were encouraging to newcomers like herself who had only been in the business as long as anyone could remember. George Burns, a 1975 winner for *The Sunshine Boys*, said that he hadn't made a film in thirty-five years, but that if

At the Academy Award ceremonies for 1948 (left to right): Douglas Fairbanks, Jr., accepting the Best Actor Award for Laurence Olivier (HAMLET); Claire Trevor, Best Supporting Actress for KEY LARGO; Jerry Wald, winner of the Irving G. Thalberg Memorial Award; Jane Wyman, Best Actress for JOHNNY BELINDA, and Walter Huston, Best Supporting Actor for THE TREASURE OF THE SIERRA MADRE.

this was the way it went, he would make another one in thirty-five more years. Burns had beaten out all competition in the best supporting actor category—which was no small trick, since any one of the others could have been his grandson.

The "I Deserve It Because I'm Old" award can backfire. No actor in Hollywood is more respected and popular than Fred Astaire, surely one of the greatest film talents of all time. His nomination at age 74 for best supporting actor in *The Towering Inferno* looked like an inevitable win, but Astaire lost to youngster Robert DeNiro. This left Astaire sitting in the front row of the theatre accepting a musical tribute from Sammy Davis, Jr. and probably wishing that his shoes had wings on. All of which only goes to prove what Astaire fans have always known—Astaire is too young and ageless ever to receive an "I Deserve It Because I'm Old" award.

5. *Tell Everyone You Don't Want It and That If You Get It You Won't Accept It.*

This is a ploy that has worked remarkably well for George C. Scott and not so well for Marlon Brando. Although it is possible that Scott will continue to receive Oscars for the rest of his professional life, it is highly unlikely that Brando will ever receive another one, even if he plays King Kong in drag and dives off the Empire State Building into a wet sponge without a double. Uncle Oscar can be snubbed, but he can't be lectured in public.

6. *Stick to Heavy Roles*

Very few Oscars are ever awarded to comedy performances or for roles in musical films. Oscar's taste in companions runs to divorcees, alcoholics, drug addicts, deaf mutes, insanity cases, suicides, cripples, split personalities, sinners, despots, informers, ruthless politicians, child molesters, rape victims, and murderers. On the other hand, he is not at all prejudiced, being partial to Irish priests, Chinese peasants, Italian women, British kings and commoners, and bald Siamese. Generally speaking, Oscar is a solemn sort, and the odds are better for winning his heart with a dramatic role, preferably seedy.

7. *Hang in There*

Oscar respects a person who never gives up. When Julie Andrews was denied the all-important role of Eliza Doolittle in the film version of *My Fair Lady*, everyone said her chance at film stardom was lost. But Andrews hung in there, and took a role in a Walt Disney picture playing a British nanny. "That takes care of her," said her critics, but Andrews had the last laugh. As far as she was concerned, the Disney picture was supercalifragilisticexpealadocious . . . she won the Oscar for it and became a big star, too. Her replacement as Eliza, Audrey Hepburn, was not even nominated, although she did win the Fair Lady of the Century award in private life by graciously showing up at the ceremony anyway—and presenting her co-star, Rex Harrison, with his best actor award.

Susan Hayward hung in there through five nominations and five losses and finally won for *I Want To Live!*. (Deborah Kerr, on the other hand, has also been nominated five times, but still has yet to win an Oscar. Hang in there, Deborah!) Frank Sinatra revitalized his career by hanging in there and fighting for the role of Maggio in *From Here To Eternity*, the award which saved his professional life. Maximilian Schell hung in there by not losing his head and getting lost in the rushes while playing alongside the great Spencer Tracy in *Judgment At Nuremberg*. Although both men were nominated, Schell was the actual winner. Never give up is the rule where Oscar is concerned. At the very least, this policy can eventually qualify you for an old age award.

8. *Hire a Press Agent*

Occasionally players seldom heard from again in films win Oscars, largely due to spectacular publicity campaigns. How else can one account for Oscars on behalf of Rita Moreno, George Chakiris, Myoshi Umeki, Red Buttons, and Lila Kedrova?

9. *The Last Resort*

Nobody's favorite uncle is the kind of relative who leaves his money to the most unlikely candidate . . . and sometimes to the least deserving. Everyone has their own favorite example of the winner who didn't deserve it . . . or the loser who got a raw deal. For the actor who never wins . . . and for the fan whose favorite never gets to run down the aisle and thank everyone from his grandmother to his hairdresser to his former tap dancing teacher to the man who rolls his lawn . . . there is one last resort: pointing out that Oscar doesn't know what he's doing anyway. This is best done by reciting a list of famous non-winners, a list long enough to fill those long spring evenings when losers weep and winners keep: Greta Garbo, Marlene Dietrich, Irene Dunne, Henry Fonda, Cary Grant, Paul Newman, Barbara Stanwyck, Claude Rains, Thelma Ritter, William Powell, Carole Lombard, Orson Welles, Leslie Howard, Jean Arthur, John Garfield, Jean Harlow, and countless others. John Barrymore never even got a nomination! And neither did Edward G. Robinson. All things considered, it's not bad company to be in.

Where Uncle Oscar is concerned, it's best to remember that, although no one agrees with the choices, most people will agree that those who did win were for the most part capable and talented . . . even if someone else was the preferred choice that particular year. Oscar is awarded to professionals by professionals, for reasons the average person does not always understand. In other words, where a rich uncle is concerned, it's best to praise his virtues and not his faults . . . even though we can't wait to start griping about next year's show.

COMING WED. THROUGH SAT.
By Leonard Maltin

Back in the days when going to the movies meant seeing not only a feature, but a newsreel, a cartoon, and a short subject, no theater would have dreamed of omitting at least one or two Previews of Coming Attractions.

Variety was the essence of these promotional pictures or trailers, as they were called in the trade. And they were often as entertaining as the films they touted. You might see Alexander Woollcott proclaiming, "*Goodbye, Mr. Chips* is the best moving picture I have ever seen," or a major star taking time out on the set to give you the lowdown on his latest epic.

Most often the selling was done by others, however—the thundering voices on the soundtracks, or the advertising copywriters, who put their hearts and souls into the amazing title cards that flashed across the screen (the 1923 *Ben-Hur* boasted "Settings of Prodigious Luxuriousness! Lavish Grandeur! Daring Gorgeousness!").

When the trailer people ran out of adjectives, they used any word that was handy. One Republic Western asserted, "Walter Brennan is inescapable as the judge!" And Warner Brothers' all-star extravaganza *Starlift* announced, "Virginia Mayo goes native—and it's BALI nice!"

There was a standard rule for making trailers, whether the studio was MGM or some Poverty Row outfit: every film was the greatest epic ever made, every cast the most stellar ever assembled. The trailer for a 1933 Mascot serial, *The Hurricane Express*, cited "The well beloved J. Farrell MacDonald, in a masterful characterization."

The trailer entrepreneurs were idefatigable. When it came time to make a trailer for *Dr. Ehrlich's Magic Bullet*, the story of the scientist who invented a cure for syphilis, the promoters backed off from revealing exactly what the film was about. The resulting reel is full of vague references to a "wonderful discovery" and "a great man." To encourage some potential viewers who would never go to see the film if they *did* know what it was about, the title card put the words "Dr. Ehrlich's" in tiny letters and "MAGIC BULLET" over the rest of the screen. One hates to think of the disappointed patrons who went to the film expecting a science-fiction tale.

Viewers with sharp minds and retentive memories could find fleeting moments or even entire scenes in trailers that never turned up in the films themselves. In the trailer for *I Loved a Woman*, when Edward G. Robinson made an emphatic point to his board of directors, he

used the word "damn," certainly a rarity in 1933. When he said the same speech in the film, his expletive was drowned out by the sound of his fist landing on a desk.

Kirsten Flagstad sang two arias in the trailer for *The Big Broadcast of 1938* . . . but only one remained in the film. Years later, when Warner Brothers decided to trim *A Star is Born*, they didn't bother to take a glimpse of a deleted song by Judy Garland out of the trailer.

Many of these discrepancies were unintentional, and some were created simply because producers had the "out-takes" and alternate negatives cut up for use in the coming-attractions reels to avoid any tampering with the precious original.

Other times, however, the clever filmmakers and promotion men who worked on trailers found ways to deliberately mislead an audience, promising something the film couldn't deliver, or focusing on merely one aspect of a wide-ranging movie. One of the oldest tricks was to re-issue a movie in which a star appeared in a supporting or even minor role, and re-alter the trailer to make him appear to be the lead character. A frequent victim of this treatment was Alan Ladd, who worked in many low-budget films before attaining stardom in the early forties. Later that decade, after the rousing success of *The Jolson Story*, Warner Brothers reissued the 1935 *Go Into Your Dance* and built the entire trailer around Jolson, completely neglecting to mention co-star (and then wife) Ruby Keeler.

Trailers were also quick to latch onto some topical angle to sell a movie, whether it was a late-breaking news story that complemented the appeal of the film or something as unique as the on-the-set friction during the making of Warners' *Manpower*, in which screen rivals George Raft and Edward G. Robinson really started punching each other, landing on many newspaper front-pages around the country. When it came time to make the trailer, Warners didn't ignore the item but instead tried to milk its publicity value by referring to the fight scenes that "had the news wires sizzling!"

Endorsement—by stars, directors, or public figures—was another tried-and-true format for "selling" a movie. The hiring of Alexander Woollcott to talk about *Goodbye Mr. Chips* was not a rarity: composer Franz Lehar appeared on-screen in 1934 to salute MGM on its remake of his *Merry Widow* . . . reporter Eric Sevareid, in newsreel fashion, spoke of the timeliness of Warners'

Edward G. Robinson in DR. EHRLICH'S MAGIC BULLET (1940). The trailer de-emphasized the good doctor, stressed the magic bullet.

1941 movie *Underground*, while Quentin Reynolds found great significance (for some obscure reason) in that same studio's fluffy comedy, *Janie*, three years later.

Still, the most successful "endorsements" of all were done in-person by the stars. Even the biggest names appeared in coming-attractions reels, as when Humphrey Bogart told a group of reporters on the set of the comedy *All Through the Night*, "I used to be a pretty tough hombre, but not any more." before describing his new picture. Bogie also participated in a sly joke for the trailer to another, more famous film. In a setting of the Hollywood Public Library, an unnamed Bogart tells a helpful young librarian that he's looking for a good mystery, "something offbeat like *The Maltese Falcon*." She suggests Raymond Chandler's new book, *The Big Sleep*, and an interested Bogie starts to read aloud as the actual coming-attractions montage begins.

In the late thirties and through the forties, Warners had the liveliest trailers of all, with an apparently bottomless bag of tricks from which to draw new ideas. The trailer for James Cagney's *The Strawberry Blonde* was presented as a Gay Nineties sing-along to "The Band Played On" ("We in-vite all you people who want to have fun to see Straw-berry Blonde . . .")'

The promotional words for Errol Flynn's *The Sea Hawk* were written on a huge sail of a vintage sailing vessel. The *Tovarich* trailer featured a series of vignettes showing various couples threatening to break up if the reluctant mate didn't agree to see the Charles Boyer-Claudette Colbert comedy. "It's *Tovarich* tonight or I'll walk," threatens a newlywed bride.

By far Warners' most successful series of trailers involved the menacing Sydney Greenstreet, who made his talking screen debut in the classic *Maltese Falcon* in 1941. Someone devised the riveting idea of spotlighting Greenstreet (then an unfamiliar face) against a black background, as he says stealthily, "Come closer! I have a story to tell you!" The "come closer" format was so successful that Greenstreet continued to appear in the trailers of such later films as *Mask of Dimitrios* and *Three Strangers*, in both of which he co-starred with Peter Lorre.

In contrast to stars on-screen, unseen hands at studio typewriters kept the trailers filled to the brim with stirring sales-pitches, a few choice examples of which we recall with pleasure:

George Arliss in *The Man Who Played God*: "More lovable! More human! More charming than ever!"

Alfred Lunt and Lynn Fontanne in *The Guardsman*: "It tickled blasé Broadway for one year."

Gold Diggers of 1933: "The musical masterpiece of the age."

Abbott and Costello *In The Navy*: "They'll torpedo your troubles and blitz your blues."

Shepherd of the Hills with John Wayne: "Until he fulfills his oath to kill, he must put aside all thoughts of love."

Some directors and producers, however, were not content to leave the promotion of their films to advertising specialists who usually handled this department. Three such filmmakers left their personal imprint on even coming-attractions reels: Orson Welles, Cecil B. DeMille, and Alfred Hitchcock.

Welles created a coming-attractions trailer for *Citizen Kane* that is as much a Welles movie as the feature itself. It opens with the Mercury Theatre microphone swinging toward the camera so that "your obedient servant" can introduce the many Mercury players making their debuts in *Kane* (Joseph Cotten, Agnes Moorehead, Dorothy Comingore, Everett Sloane, *et al.*).

When it comes to Kane himself, (played by Welles), the narrator decides to let the film's characters describe the man for us. There follows a brilliant succession of vignettes showing the *dramatis personae* of the story, each brightly lit against stark black backgrounds, speaking on the phone about Charles Foster Kane. The contrast of their comments grows stronger as the cutting accelerates between each shot, making this five-minute promotional film a small marvel of editing skill.

Equally interesting is Welles' tongue-in-cheek attitude toward the whole idea of doing a coming-attractions presentation. A shot of chorus girls in tights is included in the reel, Welles explains ruefully, as part of what is called "ballyhoo."

No such modesty could be credited to Cecil B. DeMille, who usually hosted and/or narrated his own coming attractions, bringing his great booming voice and theatrical manner to the fore—and trading on his unique reputation with the moviegoing public as Hollywood's premier filmmaker.

Who else could insist that the audience notice the resemblance between Charlton Heston and a statue of Moses carved by Michelangelo? Or declare that Paulette Goddard and Ray Milland—who just happened to be under contract to Paramount—were the ideal choices to cast

The improbable but unforgettable violin number from GOLD DIGGERS OF 1933, hailed in the trailer as "the musical masterpiece of the age."

in his story, *Reap the Wild Wind*?

From his on-screen "office"—which seemed to change for every trailer—DeMille delighted in displaying various relics and props associated with his latest production, insuring either the accuracy or validity of the endeavor.

DeMille also participated in an unusual promotional reel for *The Crusades*, a Paramount short called *Hollywood Extra Girl*. The film purported to show a typical day in the life of a struggling young "extra," Suzanne Emery, who catches the Great Man's eye and gets her big break when he decides to use her in a closeup during a crowd scene. While explaining the difficulties a young girl like Suzanne has to face, since major roles are given only to actors with broad stage experience, the narrator is impelled to add that *The Crusades*' two female stars—Loretta Young and Katherine DeMille (the director's daughter, no less!)—are exceptions to the rule, having never appeared on a stage in their lives.

While DeMille implanted his image on the American consciousness throughout his career, Alfred Hitchcock first became a celebrity in the fifties, when, as host of his own weekly television show, he established the Hitchcock style of using a dry, humorous delivery to relate macabre or suspenseful events. This has since served him well as star of his own coming-attractions, including a memorable reel plugging *Psycho*.

The trailer is particular fun if you've already seen the movie, since Hitchcock underplays the eeriness of the setting in which the story takes place. As he gives us a guided tour of the Bates Motel and hilltop home, he nonchalantly points out the spots where various brutal murders took place. Clinically describing the gore that transpired, he gets carried away with his own story and tells us, "Oh, it was ghastly!" The joke, of course, is on us, because this ghastliness wasn't real, but part of a movie which *he* directed!

A few years later, Hitchcock reappeared on-screen to promote *The Birds*, isolating one of the black-feathered friends in a cage in his office, only to have the bird peck at his hand in the course of his speech.

Men like Hitchcock, DeMille, and Welles didn't have to resort to hyperbole to claim their films as unique. Their very presence in the coming-attractions trailers told the audience just that—while other movies' non-stop use of superlatives made it difficult for moviegoers to separate fact from fancy.

Yet somehow the trailers themselves became part of the fun of that Golden Age; they transcended their advertis-

CITIZEN KANE (1941). With Dorothy Comingore and Orson Welles. The trailer was a feature in itself.

ing pose to become an integral (and enjoyable) part of the movie program.

And if they oversold their wares from time to time—well, that was a part of the era, too. Who could seriously quibble with a promotion man's claim for the 1923 *Ben-Hur* that there was "nothing like it before—perhaps never again?" The same kind of copy-writers for *Dr. Ehrlich's Magic Bullet* underestimated the staying-power of movies in their own attempt to sell *that* film, declaring, "Ten years from now it will still be remembered!"

And that was more than thirty years ago.

EXTRY! EXTRY!

Each of the following "headlines" refers to the plot—or a crucial incident in the plot—of a particular film.

How many of the films can you identify? (It was a curious device of many old movies to further the story line with a banner headline that would normally make the back page of a newspaper—"HEIRESS RUNS OFF WITH AVIATOR!," etc.)

1. BEDLAM IN THE AUTOMAT!—CROWDS BATTLE FOR FREE FOOD AS ALL SLOTS OPEN!

2. LEO MINOSA STILL TRAPPED IN CAVE! CROWDS GATHER TO WATCH RESCUE. (Exclusive story by Charles Tatum)

3. SMALL-TOWN GIRL HAS SEXTUPLETS! FATHER NORVAL JONES DECLARED HERO!

4. MERCY PLANE RACING WITH SERUM TO SAVE MASON BABY. PARENTS PRAY.

5. EX-MOVIE STAR BLANCHE HUDSON FOUND NEAR DEATH ON BEACH. SISTER QUESTIONED.

6. THE TRUE STORY!: HOW UNDERCOVER ARMY "DESERTER" FOILED JAPANESE SNEAK ATTACK ON CANAL ZONE DEFENSES—Rick Leland's Full Story!

7. MANDERLEY DESTROYED BY FIRE! Housekeeper apparently only victim.

8. EXCLUSIVE! AD EXECUTIVE ROGER THORNHILL TELLS HOW HE UNCOVERED SPY RING THROUGH MISTAKEN IDENTITY!

9. NEWS FROM HOLLYWOOD: BABY "HAPPY" ACCLAIMED AS "AMERICA'S SWEETEST SWEETHEART" IN FIRST MOVIE. Proud mother at premiere.

10. WHERE WILL "THE NECKTIE KILLER" STRIKE NEXT? LATEST VICTIM FOUND IN BACK OF POTATO TRUCK.

11. WHO IS GLADYS GLOVER? BILLBOARD AROUSES SPECULATION ABOUT MYSTERY WOMAN.

12. READ "MY LIFE AS A JEW"—PHIL GREEN'S SCORCHING EXPOSE OF ANTI-SEMITISM IN AMERICA!

13. FRANK SKEFFINGTON DEFEATED IN FINAL BID FOR MAYORALTY! "I'm sorry the show didn't have a happy ending," he tells staff.

14. KINGPIN GANGSTER JOHNNY ROCCO SLAIN IN FLORIDA SHOOTOUT! Held group hostage in hotel.

15. RUSSIAN SUBMARINE GOES AGROUND ON ISLAND OFF CAPE COD! ISLANDERS UP IN ARMS!

16. PSYCHIATRIST MURDERED! Are police suppressing bizarre evidence of wild beast at large?

17. SOCIETY SCOOP!: TRACY LORD REMARRIES EX C. DEXTER HAVEN IN SURPRISE CEREMONY!

18. THOUSANDS ATTEND FUND-RAISING RALLY FOR ANGEL CHAVEZ! BARNEY SLOANE KEY SPEAKER.

19. STAGE NEWS: LILY GARLAND TRIUMPHS IN STAGE DEBUT! ("She's my greatest protégé," says Oscar Jaffe.)

20. "I'M INNOCENT!," BARBARA GRAHAM CRIES, AS SHE IS LED TO EXECUTION.

(Answers on page 152)

Bonus Photo Question:
A possible headline for the above scene: "DANCE HALL "HOSTESS" MARY DWIGHT TELLS ALL IN COURTROOM! D.A. David Graham promises more revelations!" Name the movie.

AREN'T WE
ANGELS/DEVILS?

Over the years, confronted with the necessity of depicting visions of heaven and hell, the Hollywood studios have scrupulously avoided controversy by resorting to whimsy and fantasy. Heaven is usually shown as a quaint place of billowing clouds, inhabited by benign angels who, when they're not busy playing harps, enjoy assuming mortal form for plot purposes. And until Hollywood discovered diabolism as a popular subject, Satan was usually characterized as a devilishly charming and suave rascal, rather than a fire-breathing ogre.

This quiz is concerned with filmdom's angels and devils over the years. You may be surprised at some of the forms they've taken.

A scene from Warners' 1936 film version of Marc Connelly's fable, THE GREEN PASTURES. At a fish fry in heaven, De Lawd (Rex Ingram) is greeted by his angels.

1. Name the movies in which each of the following actors played an angel: a) Cary Grant b) Henry Travers, and c) Clifton Webb.

2. One of Ernst Lubitsch's deftest comedies of the forties was *Heaven Can Wait*. It concerned an elderly gentleman of rakish behavior who reviewed his life for the benefit of Lucifer (here called "His Excellency"). Who played this gentleman, and who played Lucifer?

3. Name the *two* films in which Edward Everett Horton played an angel called Messenger 7013.

4. In *A Guy Named Joe* (1943), when pilot Spencer Tracy dies in a crash, he goes off to MGM heaven. Who turns up as the Commanding General of dead aviators: a) Lewis Stone b) Reginald Owen, or c) Lionel Barrymore?

5. In which movie did each of the following actresses play an envoy or disciple of the Devil: a) Gwen Verdon b) Simone Simon, and c) Patsy Kelly?

6. Name the films in which James Mason and Fred Astaire played "guardian angels," one genuine (Mason), one fraudulent (Astaire).

7. The word "angel" has been used in many movie titles without heavenly connotation—more as a term of endearment. For example, can you name the movie in which:

   a) Loretta Young has sleepwalking problems.
   b) Herbert Marshall and Melvyn Douglas vie for Marlene Dietrich's affections.
   c) Peter Ustinov plays an escapee from Devil's Island?

8. In a 1947 film, Robert Cummings played Archangel Michael, sent to earth to set matters right in a Western mining town. Was the film called a) *For Heaven's Sake* b) *Heaven Only Knows* or c) *Heavens Above*?

9. The Devil has been known by many names. In which movie was he called a) Nick Beal b) the Dark Hermit, and c) Applegate?

10. In the movie *Angels in the Outfield* (1951), who played the baseball manager who is helped to win the pennant for his team through heavenly intervention? Was it a) Paul Douglas b) Edward G. Robinson, or c) William Bendix?

11. Name the actors who played the title roles in *I Married An Angel* (1942).

12. Each of the following movies has a "devilish" or "hellish" reference in its title. Can you name them?

   a) Working girl Jean Arthur believes that wealthy boss Charles Coburn is a down-and-outer.
   b) Lee Marvin and Toshiro Mifune are trapped together on a deserted island during World War II.
   c) Devil's Island escapee Lionel Barrymore shrinks humans to doll-size.
   d) Marlene Dietrich plays a seductive wench named Concha Perez.
   e) The star: Spencer Tracy. The most famous scene: a startling vision of Satan's domain.

13. *Outward Bound* (1930) dealt with a group of passengers aboard a ship who discover that they're dead and on their way to another world. Can you name the Warners' 1944 remake of this film?

14. In the British film, *The Angel Who Pawned Her Harp* (1956)—she does, literally, to pay for her earthly expenses—the title role was played by a) Diane Cilento b) Jean Simmons, or c) Glynis Johns?

15. That splendid actor Claude Rains played a heavenly type in one movie and a devilish type in another. Can you name the two films?

16. In 1942, Robert Young played *Joe Smith, American*, a patriotic factory worker. Eight years later, Joe, now played by James Whitmore, returned with his wife and son in an MGM fantasy. In this movie, Joe hears God speak to him over the radio, calling on mankind to create miracles of kindness, goodness, and peace. (Yes, that's the plot.) Can you name the movie?

17. Name the film in which each of the following actors sold his soul to the Devil: a) Dudley Moore b) James Craig, and c) Richard Burton.

18. Devil worship has always been a popular film subject. Name the movie in which:

   a) David Niven resorts to some black magic to get his failing vineyards back to health.
   b) Kim Hunter discovers that her sister is involved with a devil-cult.
   c) Shirley MacLaine discovers that her brother is possessed by demons and is a homicidal menace.

19. Name the "heavenly" film in which each of the following characters plays a prominent role: a) Little Joe Jackson b) Alexander Levine, and c) Count Palaffi.

20. Sometimes a character in a film conveniently *dreams* that he's being transported to his heavenly reward. In which film did this happen to Jack Benny?

(Answers on page 152)

CHUCKLES AND GUFFAWS

Each item below refers to a moment, incident, or scene in a well-known comedy movie. How many of the movies can you name?

1. Charles Coburn cries, "Damn the torpedoes! Full steam ahead!"

2. Ginger Rogers is given instruction in "military maneuvers" by a group of eager young cadets.

3. Jack Lemmon strains his spaghetti with a tennis racket.

4. Mary Boland tells a teary, woebegone Joan Fontaine, "My dear, you've got the Reno jumpie-wumpies!"

5. Bette Davis kisses James Cagney, then jumps back shrieking, "Mustard!"

6. Trying to get some sleep on his porch, W. C. Fields is interrupted by a man looking for "Karl La Fong."

7. Roscoe Karns comments on John Barrymore: "He won't shoot himself. It would please too many people."

8. Marilyn Monroe is introduced by George Sanders as a graduate of "the Copacabana School of Dramatic Art."

9. Inadvertently, a sticker reading "Lern the Big Apple —10¢" gets attached to Jean Arthur's dress.

10. Not knowing that wife Doris Day has had a pool built on their property, James Garner blithely drives his car into the water—and sinks.

11. In her kitchen, Katharine Hepburn grapples with eggs that slide off the counter, coffee that boils over, and waffles that rise almost to the ceiling.

12. Describing her wayward husband on the witness stand, Judy Holliday says, "He used to not do that a lot—come home."

13. Irene Dunne does a rowdy version (with uplifted skirt) of a song called "Gone With the Wind."

14. Pretending to be demented, William Powell "frees" his feet from his shoes, in the manner of Lincoln freeing the slaves.

15. Peter Sellers hears a woman shriek behind a door, rushes through the door past a trilling soprano—and out a second story window.

16. Succumbing to an urge to kiss ZaSu Pitts, Charles Laughton says, "I coarsely gave way to the brute in me."

17. Hauled into court for disorderly conduct, Barbra Streisand discovers that the judge is her father.

18. Carl Reiner and Tessie O'Shea, bound together back to back, try frantically to get down a flight of stairs.

19. The film's last shot: a man marching with a sandwich board that reads "Buljanoff and Iranoff Unfair to Kopalski."

20. Jack Lemmon squeals joyfully to Tony Curtis, "I'm engaged!"

21. Roscoe Karns tells Claudette Colbert, "Shapeley's the name, and that's the way I like 'em."

22. Katharine Hepburn tells Cary Grant about her house: "It's haunted by ghosts wearing stuffed shirts and mink-lined ties."

23. In a ship's cabin, poor Henry Fonda is overcome by Barbara Stanwyck's perfume, all the while telling her that his main interest is snakes.

24. Dressed in a frilly negligee, Cary Grant tells a startled May Robson, "I went *gay* all of a sudden!"

25. On a hill overlooking a town, a divorce lawyer removes a baton from his attaché case, and "conducts" a series of marital squabbles.

(Answers on page 152)

One of the greatest guffaw-producing scenes in film history: the uproarious stateroom scene from A NIGHT AT THE OPERA (1935), with the Marx Brothers in full bloom.

LINES TO REMEMBER

How many of the following lines of dialogue from well-known films can you identify? And can you recall the players who spoke them?

1. "Mister, what does it mean when a man says, 'I'm crashing out'?"
2. "You always said you could shoot. And I never believed you."
3. "Marry me, and I'll never look at another horse!"
4. "It took more than one man to change my name to Shanghai Lily."
5. "I never drink *wine* . . ."
6. "Wasn't I lucky to be born in my favorite city?"
7. "I'm the one that has to do the singing. I'm the one that gets the razzberries."
8. "That's the kind of hairpin I am!"
9. "Always the same. People come. People go. Nothing ever happens."
10. "May I have this dance, Mother?"
11. "I hate you! Without a shred of pity, without a shred of regret, I watch you go with glory in my heart!"
12. "I killed you! Haunt me then! Haunt your murderer!"
13. "I make more money than Calvin Coolidge put together!"
14. "A woman is beautiful only when she is loved."
15. "Today, I consider myself the luckiest man on the face of the earth."
16. "Walking with you through life, ma'am, has been a very gracious thing."
17. "Put me in your pocket, Mike."
18. "Money! Money! The Frankenstein monster that destroys souls!"
19. "What a greedy girl you are. You want so much of everything."
20. "The only question I ever ask any woman is, 'What time is your husband coming home?'"
21. "In my opinion, you are not only sane, you are the sanest man who ever walked into this courtroom."
22. "Modern methods! Poppycock! Give a boy a sense of humor and a sense of proportion and he'll stand up to anything."
23. "Every once in a while I suddenly find myself dancing."
24. "You not only put the love of God into them, you scared the hell out of them!"
25. "It was a toss-up whether I go in for diamonds or sing in the choir. The choir lost."

(Answers on page 152)

THE MANY FACES OF A PRIVATE EYE
By Curtis F. Brown

As a qualified movie buff, you should be able to answer the following question right off the top of your fact-filled head. What do these players have in common: George Kuwa, Sojin, E. L. Park, Warner Oland, Sidney Toler, and Roland Winters? You're right, the last three names are the giveaway. Between 1926 and 1949, they all played Earl Derr Biggers' philosophical Oriental sleuth, Charlie ("Words cannot cook rice") Chan.

Another warm-up teaser or two before we get down to business. Between 1937 and 1939, Peter Lorre played him in eight pictures; Henry Silva portrayed him once, in 1965; and in between, Porky Pig—th-th-that's right!—did the honors in 1939. Who is he? Of course, he's Mr. Moto, novelist J. P. Marquand's delightful jiu jitsu expert and nemesis of miscreants. (Do you remember *Porky's Movie Mystery*, a cartoon short that playfully satirized the likeable—pre-Pearl Harbor—Japanese crime fighter?)

Just one more before the big one. From 1939 into the forties, which two actors played Michael Shayne, mystery writer Brett Halliday's popular sleuth? You're correct if you guessed Lloyd Nolan (in the first seven of those thrillers), and you deserve the Shillelagh Award if you remembered that Hugh Beaumont succeeded Nolan in the final five entries in the series.

Now for the Main Event. Before you rest too comfortably on your laurels, try these unlikely combinations of actors. What single character did two Montgomerys, Robert and George, play on the screen? Dick Powell and Elliott Gould? Humphrey Bogart, James Garner, Robert Mitchum? And, with some fudging, George Sanders and Lloyd Nolan?

All nine actors relate, to a greater or lesser extent, to Philip Marlowe, one of the great detectives of mystery fiction and the most variously portrayed of the cinema shamuses. Of that number, mystery-movie buffs would grant top honors to Dick Powell and Humphrey Bogart for their nearly model, though differing, characterizations of the wisecracking, gruff, sardonic yet basically idealistic loner.

Philip Marlowe, novelist Raymond Chandler's medium hard-boiled private investigator, undertakes single-handedly to expose crime and metropolitan corruption where the police fear—or refuse—to tread. He has no efficient and adoring secretary such as Effie Perine, whom Dashiell Hammett furnished to Sam Spade; no Number One Son; no comic-relief stooge to do the heavy work;

and neither doting girl friend nor dotty wife to supply well-intentioned but zany solutions such as those Nora Charles proffered Nick, her lighthearted detective husband in the *Thin Man* series.

Using their looks, personality, and talent, most screen Marlowes have at least suggested Chandler's own vision of a man "who is not himself mean, who is neither tarnished nor afraid. . . . A man of honor—by instinct, by inevitability, without thought of it, and certainly without saying. . . . The best man in his world and a good enough man for any world. . . . [who] talks as the man of his age talks—that is, with rude wit, a lively sense of the grotesque, a disgust for sham and a contempt for pettiness."

Thus Chandler set a difficult target to hit, one that actors have either missed by a mile, fallen short of by yards, or—rarely—hit squarely in the bull's eye.

Let's see how the movie Marlowes have fared.

In 1941, John Huston's masterly adaptation and direction of Hammett's *The Maltese Falcon* gave new life to the private-eye film, a genre that had generally deteriorated into flattened out *Thin Man* entries—despite the retention of William Powell and Myrna Loy in the principal parts—and "who cares?" whodunits with the last of the gentlemanly Vances, courteous Chans, and the rest. Thanks in large part to Bogart's superbly etched portrayal of Spade in *The Maltese Falcon*, mystery melodramas were acquiring a welcome look and sound of reality.

A year after *The Maltese Falcon*'s release, RKO offered a programmer, *The Falcon Takes Over*, the first "Marlowe" picture. It presented a hybrid offspring of Michael Arlen's modern-day Robin Hood, The Falcon, and only obliquely Chandler's Philip Marlowe. *Farewell, My Lovely*, that author's second novel, published in 1940, furnished only the story, with George Sanders playing his accustomed suave, slightly supercilious Falcon, a far cry from the morose man Chandler saw as "always in a lonely street, in lonely rooms, puzzled but never quite defeated."

In 1942, the year of Sanders' Marlowe-as-Falcon, Twentieth Century-Fox released *Time to Kill*. This time, Chandler's *The High Window* provided the bare bones of the film's plot. Again, the Marlowe character was "masked," this time as Michael Shayne, Brett Halliday's tough-guy shamus, a role Lloyd Nolan had played half a dozen times before. The character was pure Shayne, an

MURDER, MY SWEET (1944). With Mike Mazurki, Otto Kruger, and Dick Powell

entertaining but not very interesting defender of the law. The portrayal reflected Nolan's properly hearty, cocksure conception of Shayne, not Chandler's often bitter hero-detective, for whom his creator once expressed an affinity: "Marlowe and I do not despise the upper classes because they take baths and have money; we despise them because they are phoney."

In the two years that passed before anything like a "real" Philip Marlowe reached the screen, large numbers of crime-fiction buffs as well as those interested in "literature" had heeded the critical acclaim for Chandler's novels as they appeared—first *The Big Sleep* (1939), followed by *Farewell, My Lovely* (1940) and *The High Window* (1942). As a result, they became intimately familiar with Marlowe's ways and appearance as Chandler described him in those works. Far from George Sanders' cosmopolitan Falcon or the one-dimensional private dick of Lloyd Nolan's Michael Shayne, Chandler's creation was a fully realized husky, brown-eyed, 190-pound, over six-footer, nearly forty years old, single, and attractive to women. He had gone to college, could "still speak English if there's any demand for it," lived in a modest three-and-a-half room apartment at the Hobart Arms on Los Angeles' Franklin Avenue. He worked out of a small,

shabby office (furnished with a desk, phone, swivel chair, and, for clients, "three near-walnut chairs") on the sixth floor of the Cahuenga Building on Hollywood Boulevard for $25 a day (later raised to $40) and expenses ("when I'm lucky," and then "mostly for gasoline and whiskey.").

This was the image of the man that future actors cast as Marlowe would try to project.

The first pure Philip Marlowe film was *Murder, My Sweet* (1944), screenwriter John Paxton's gratifyingly faithful adaptation of *Farewell, My Lovely*. This time, RKO atoned for *The Falcon Takes Over*. Edward Dmytryk's direction is crisp, swift-paced, imaginative, and redolent of the strangely ominous atmosphere of Los Angeles, a city that, according to Chandler, seems carefree and innocent only to those who know it superficially. Above all, the offbeat casting of Dick Powell—neither husky nor tall, but catching just the right tone of Marlowe's surface insouciance—in the central role brought to the screen the first genuinely Chandlerian movie. Previously associated with Busby Berkeley musicals and second-rate frothy comedies, Powell more than rises to the challenge in his depiction of the sardonic but tenacious Marlowe. In fact, the actor's still-boyish appearance en-

27

THE BIG SLEEP (1946). With Humphrey Bogart and Lauren Bacall

hanced his characterization of Chandler's "untarnished" hero.

Entwined in a typically complex Chandler plot, stemming from a Neanderthal ex-con's search for his former girl friend, Marlowe is nearly murdered by the rich and decadent Mrs. Grayle, totally committed to keeping her wealth intact and her past hidden. Mike Mazurki as the near-moronic Moose Malloy; Claire Trevor as the ruthlessly scheming Mrs. Grayle (whom Malloy recalls as being "as cute as lace pants"), now married to a multimillionaire; and Gladys George as Mrs. Florian, a drunken slattern who holds the key to Mrs. Grayle's past—all helped make *Murder, My Sweet* a standard by which succeeding Marlowe films would be measured. Not surprisingly, however, a concession was made to Hollywood convention at the final fade-out when Powell and Anne Shirley, as the evil Mrs. Grayle's stepdaughter, are linked romantically.

While the film version of his first novel, *The Big Sleep*, was being readied for release in mid-1946, Chandler wrote to his British publisher, "Bogart can be tough without a gun. Also he has a sense of humor that contains that grating undertone of contempt. Bogart is the genuine article." As close as Powell had come to bringing Marlowe

to life on the screen, Warner Bros.' enlistment of Humphrey Bogart, the studio's foremost male star at the time, seemed then and still does to many Marlowe watchers a "dream" casting.

When *The Big Sleep* was filmed (from late 1944 into 1945), Bogart was about five years older than Marlowe; Powell was an apt thirty-eight for *Murder, My Sweet*. Although Bogart, like Powell, was no six-footer, the script deals adroitly with the fact. When Carmen Sternwood (Martha Vickers), General Sternwood's degenerate daughter, meets Marlowe for the first time she comments: "You're not very tall, are you?" The detective shows a sense of humor containing the "grating undertone of contempt" that Chandler perceived in Bogart when he turns aside the put-down with, "Well, I tried to be." (In the novel, Marlowe's height prompts Carmen to observe, "Tall, aren't you?" Marlowe counters with an ironic, "I didn't mean to be.")

The screenplay, by William Faulkner, Leigh Brackett, and Jules Furthman, has baffled even the most alert film commentators and film-goers from the time of its initial showing to its many subsequent revivals. Although the writers were faced with a heavy task in transferring to the screen Chandler's formidably involved and densely populated plot, they nevertheless accomplished a tour de force in their superb adaptation, having to concede only two major points to studio demands. One, a smouldering attraction between Marlowe and Carmen's overly protective sister, Vivian (Lauren Bacall), introduces a stabilizing element of conventionality into a story involving pornography, drug addiction, homosexuality, and nymphomania, in addition to more standard fare of blackmail and murder. The other was switching the killer of Sean Regan, oil-wealthy General Sternwood's trusted companion, from a vengeful Carmen (who, in the novel, shoots Regan for rebuffing her persistent advances) to racketeer Eddie Mars (John Ridgely). In the film, Mars has murdered Regan; he then blackmails Vivian, having easily convinced her that her deranged sister committed the crime. Admittedly, Marlowe's solution of Regan's murder is eliptical and is delivered at lightning speed within the last few minutes of the movie.

Warners lavished some of its best talents on *The Big Sleep*. In addition to its fast-moving script, much of the tangy dialogue coming straight from Chandler's text, Sid Hickox's shadowy camera work and Max Steiner's richly thematic score, Howard Hawks' taut direction of a first-rate cast is still studied and admired today for its dextrous blending of dark decadence and mint-bright super-sophisticated exchanges between Bogart and Bacall. The actor's rather seedy appearance contrasts artfully with his faintly superior air of amused disdain for the sordid predicaments in which the "phoney" rich land themselves. Even at his most laconic, he seems to express whole sentences, as when Vivian grandly reminds Marlowe that "People don't talk like that to me," adding

LADY IN THE LAKE (1946). With Robert Montgomery and Audrey Totter

"Do you always think you can handle people like trained seals?" The shamus' reply is a simple "Uh-huh. I usually get away with it, too." So nearly does Bogart become Marlowe as Chandler describes him that it's almost impossible to read the novels without "hearing" the distinctive Bogart voice throughout the first-person narratives.

One can regard only with dismay the next two attempts to bring Marlowe's special qualities to the screen. MGM's *Lady in the Lake*, based on Chandler's fourth novel, published in 1943, was released in 1946, the same year as *The Big Sleep*. It could have been a respectable contender in the Marlowe-on-film canon but for a fatal misjudgment on director-star Robert Montgomery's part as to how the story should be visualized.

Chandler's stories are labyrinthine and demand extraordinary attention from the reader. But motion pictures don't permit going back a few pages to clarify a point. If a viewer misses an important bit of action or exchange of dialogue, he becomes hopelessly lost in the plot's maze of false leads, sudden turns, intricate motivations. Montgomery, by opting for a camera-as-Marlowe technique during virtually the entire film, obliges the other players to address and react to the camera. The effect is that they are delivering their lines directly to the movie audience, not the unseen Marlowe. By the very nature of its distracting treatment, *Lady in the Lake* fails to engross its viewers in Chandler's crackling—and characteristically convoluted—plot involving drownings, disguises, and a murderous cop. Nevertheless, the movie was ambitiously conceived, expensively mounted, and excellently cast with capable performers such as Audrey Totter, Jayne Meadows, Tom Tully, and Lloyd Nolan as the principal villain.

The exception is Montgomery, whose refined voice (we glimpse him in mirrors and in a few scenes of narration) doesn't suit a shamus working for $25 a day and expenses. The film is undramatic, done in by its cleverness. Significantly, Chandler himself withdrew from the chore of adapting his novel, allowing Steve Fisher, his collaborator, to take sole screen credit.

Just as RKO had filmed the story of *Farewell, My Lovely* twice, the first time without Marlowe and again as the memorable *Murder, My Sweet*, so Twentieth Century-Fox took two turns at *The High Window*, as the non-Marlowe *Time to Kill* and later as *The Brasher Doubloon* (1947). Neither imaginatively conceived, like *Lady in the Lake*, nor richly atmospheric like *Murder, My Sweet* or *The Big Sleep*, *The Brasher Doubloon* suffered

THE BRASHER DOUBLOON (1947). With George Montgomery and Nancy Guild

MARLOWE (1969). With James Garner in the title role

principally from John Brahm's stolid direction and George Montgomery's energetic Philip Marlowe. (In addition, Montgomery's voice has an unsettling similarity to Clark Gable's.) Walking away with the picture was Florence Bates, a majestic character actress, whose gorgon of a dowager, Mrs. Murdock, is worth remembering if only for her grand-scale nastiness toward her personal secretary, Merle Davis, played with fitting mousiness by Nancy Guild.

In Dorothy Hannah's screenplay, based on Leonard Praskin's adaptation of *The High Window*, the private eye has two interests: pursuing Merle Davis, who has been tricked by Mrs. Murdock into believing that she murdered her employer's first husband, and investigating the mysterious disappearance of a rare gold coin. The movie's one imaginative touch is substituting the novel's crucial, if fortuitous, snapshots, which prove Mrs. Murdock pushed her husband out of his office window to his death, with a motion picture of the crime. George Montgomery is Marlowe's height and age, but his brisk manner and trim turn-out do not conjure up Philip Marlowe.

Over twenty years passed before Hollywood took on Marlowe again. In 1969, MGM brought Chandler's fifth novel, *The Little Sister* (1949), to the screen as, simply, *Marlowe*. This time the private eye, in the person of James Garner, is just about the right age and build for the shamus as Chandler saw him. Stirling Silliphant's screenplay acceptably updated the novel, peopling some scenes with strung-out hippies to lend it a "with-it" dash. Director Paul Bogart sees to it that the California locales—seedy rooming houses, Hollywood sound stages, airports—are given their picturesque due in veteran William H. Daniels' color photography. But the film also caters to an American taste for displays of violence, and there are too many gratuitous gag lines.

Garner plays Marlowe almost exclusively for laughs as he investigates the strange disappearance of Orrin Quest (Robert Newman), brother of "little sister" Orfamay Quest (Sharon Farrell). Generally, Garner assumes a baffled air, coupled with a swagger born more of a boyish show of confidence than of Marlowe's seasoned self-

THE LONG GOODBYE (1973). With Sterling Hayden, Elliott Gould, Nina Van Pallandt, and Henry Gibson

assurance. His style is basically that of Dick Powell's appealing chipper-whatever-the-odds attitude taken several steps further, rather than the more persuasive—and more interesting—tradition of Bogart's, and Chandler's, man of introspection.

The Long Goodbye (1973), based on the sixth and last published Chandler novel (1953) offers the most original, if not necessarily the most successful, conception of Marlowe yet filmed. Robert Altman, a brilliant director, and Leigh Brackett, a gifted member of the writing team responsible for *The Big Sleep*, wrote the screenplay. They re-create Marlowe, presenting him as he might be in today's Los Angeles—a seductive city of blatantly luxurious tackiness and a full flowering of the corruption and amorality, on both sides of the law, that had led to Chandler's ambivalent love affair with the town in the first place.

The novel itself presents a somewhat altered Marlowe, a detective-hero whose tough skepticism has now given way to the darker moods of cynicism. Although still courageous and retaining his personal code of ethics, he sees a world that would lead him to agree with his

creator's later assessment of Los Angeles as a "tired old whore." Altman and Brackett carry this Chandler-Marlowe disenchantment several measures further by depicting Marlowe as a shabby man of the 1970s, made almost eccentric in contrast with the "well-adjusted" freaks surrounding him. The director and writer imply that Marlowe, were he around today, would be a living anachronism. He smokes unfiltered cigarettes, he has traded in his Chrysler for a 1948 Lincoln Continental convertible, and though still a loner, he has acquired—of all things for Philip Marlowe—an apathetic cat.

The movie follows the outlines of the book: the detective agrees to help an old friend, Terry Lennox (Jim Bouton), a small-time hood and full-time playboy, extricate himself from a charge of murdering his wife. Elliott Gould as the shamus whom the world, to its discredit, has passed by, lumbers, mumbles (rather too much), and is as bewildered as any man born out of his time. However, the conclusion departs radically from the novel. Lennox, guilty after all, has deceived Marlowe. The detective shoots Lennox not to protect himself, but in cold-blooded rage. Although *The Big Sleep* has Marlowe kill extortionist Eddie Mars and Canino, his trigger man, in self-defense, Lennox's treacherous exploitation of trust ("You'll never learn. You're a born loser," and "What are friends for?") pushes Marlowe to the brink of madness. The "untarnished" private eye murders the friend and client who betrayed him.

The Long Goodbye (distributed by United Artists) is an adventurous motion picture. Vilmos Zsigmond's color photography captures perfectly the drowsy, lotus-land haziness of Los Angeles, the John Williams score is sweetly sad, and a supporting cast that includes Sterling Hayden, Nina Van Pallandt, Henry Gibson, and Mark Rydell, succeeds in conveying Altman's and Brackett's theme: a man's code of honor may have remained unchanged, but the world has not. Marlowe's weapon against evil is no longer an intense personal concern but a frustrated act of private revenge. Even a public inured to violence did not accept a hero whom they believed killed wantonly, and *The Long Goodbye* did not enjoy the success many feel its bold conception deserved.

Farewell, My Lovely (Avco Embassy Pictures, 1975) is the most recent Marlowe film and the second full-scale treatment of the novel. The movie returns Marlowe to Los Angeles of the early forties, but it's a little too insistently nostalgic—radios play only songs of that time readily recognizable today and, as photographed by John Alonzo, neon signs seem not garish but like trendy art displays, and mean hallways are bathed in overly luscious tints.

Director Dick Richards, screenwriter David Zelag Goodman, and Robert Mitchum, a skilled actor of long experience, see Marlowe as a conspicuously late-middle-aged private eye, a little tired and slow, but still a man whose brushes with human aberrance leave him a little "puzzled but never quite defeated." Charlotte Rampling, cast as Mrs. Grayle (the role Claire Trevor made her own in *Murder, My Sweet*) is directed to suggest the sultry, languid Lauren Bacall of *The Big Sleep*. The effect is mildly amusing but scarcely menacing; fortunately, her scenes are too few for the "homage" to be irritating. Only Sylvia Miles' slovenly drunk, Mrs. Florian, comes up to the level of her counterpart in *Murder, My Sweet*.

Hawk-eyed movie buffs who saw *Tony Rome* (1967) and *Lady in Cement* (1968), films in which Frank Sinatra is a Marlowe-like private eye operating out of Miami, may have spotted Chandlerian situations and characters recalling *The Big Sleep*, *Farewell, My Lovely*, and other Marlowe stories. But similarities end there, as reviewers noted when the pictures were released.

Seven Marlowes—Dick Powell, Humphrey Bogart, Robert Montgomery, George Montgomery, James Garner, Elliott Gould, and Robert Mitchum. Which one do you think comes closest to Raymond Chandler's great detective-hero as the author saw him?

A final quiz question may cause you to wonder still more. In 1951 Chandler, replying to a letter from a correspondent wrote: "If I ever had an opportunity of selecting the movie actor who could best represent [Marlowe] to my mind, I think it would have been -----."

Can you supply the name? This time, you're probably wrong. The answer is Cary Grant.

Editor's Note: Would you like to test your knowledge of other movie detectives? See the photo quiz beginning on page 97.

FAREWELL, MY LOVELY (1975). Robert Mitchum as Philip Marlowe

BLESS THE BEASTS

Each of the items below refers to a particular movie in which an animal (or group of animals) played an important role. You are asked to identify the movie.

1. In a nightclub, a giant gorilla holds a girl and a piano on a platform above his head—and plays tug-of-war with famous athletes.

2. A strife-torn family on a snow-bound California ranch is in terror of a stalking panther.

3. The characters include Susan Vance, Major Applegate—and a leopard.

4. Rex Harrison sings a plaintive song—to a seal.

5. Gilian Holroyd strokes a cat named Pyewacket.

6. Entomologist Edmund Gwenn and his daughter work to destroy a breed of giant, murderous ants.

7. The story of a horse, co-starring Fred MacMurray, Anne Baxter, and the horse.

8. Tom Ewell sings to a hog named Blue Boy.

9. While Bing Crosby romances Joan Fontaine, his fox terrier romances her pet poodle.

10. A group of gorillas gets perilously close to stealing this movie from the likes of Clark Gable and Ava Gardner.

11. Terry Moore's uncle vows he'll come back to earth as a race horse. And he does!

12. A principal character in this movie is a cat wearing a wrist watch around his neck as a collar. He leads the F.B.I. to a pair of bank robbers.

13. Sandy Dennis, Anne Heywood, and Keir Dullea tangle erotically on an isolated farm. The creature of the title is symbolically involved.

14. The heroine's mother says: "Everyone should have a chance at a breathtaking piece of folly at least once in his life." The folly here is attempting to win a horse race.

15. *The New York Times* review said this movie contained "two of the most sickening sights one casual swatter-wielder ever beheld on the screen."

16. In this movie, the scene-stealers are baby elephants. And the climax is the chase after a charging rhino.

17. A murdered dog returns to earth as Dick Powell in order to find his killer.

18. The sleek feline actress Gale Sondergaard played a sleek feline named Tylette.

19. In addition to the titular hero, this film included animals named Doris and Mary Lou, and the humans included Marshall Thompson and Betsy Drake.

20. The hero of this 1969 movie was "otterly" talented.

(Answers on page 153)

Bonus Photo Question:
A gathering about the fire in TARZAN'S DESERT MYSTERY (1943), with Nancy Kelly, Johnny Sheffield, and Johnny Weissmuller. Now can you name the pensive chimpanzee?

STAGE TO SCREEN

This is a quiz that revolves about film versions of stage plays, and the players who appear in both. Sometimes the film version is an improvement on the original, sometimes a desecration of it. But here's a chance to test your knowledge of stage-to-screen transformations.

1. Name the stage (and occasional movie) star whose roles were played on screen by Ruth Hussey in *The Philadelphia Story*, Betty Field in *Tomorrow the World*, and Rosalind Russell in *My Sister Eileen*.

2. Which of the following plays by George S. Kaufman was never filmed: a) *Beggar on Horseback* b) *Once In a Lifetime* c) *The Royal Family*, or d) *Merrily We Roll Along*?

3. Rita Hayworth, Mitzi Gaynor, Gloria Grahame, and Rita Moreno all appeared in film versions of Richard Rodgers' musicals. Can you name the movie musical in which each appeared?

4. John Barrymore, Joe E. Brown, Elisabeth Bergner, Elizabeth Taylor. All starred in movie versions of plays by one writer. Name the writer—and the movies.

5. Who played Boris Karloff's role in the movie version of *Arsenic and Old Lace*? And who played Josephine Hull's stage role in the same movie?

6. Samson Raphaelson's play, *Accent on Youth*, about a playwright's romance with his secretary, was filmed in 1935 with Sylvia Sidney and Herbert Marshall and remade in 1950 as a) *Just For You* b) *Here Comes the Groom*, or c) *Mr. Music*?

7. On stage he played Peter Stuyvesant, first ruler of the island of Manhattan. On screen he played Mr. Scratch, who caused havoc in New England. Name this marvelous actor, and the play and movie in which he acted these roles.

8. The following performers have all appeared in film versions of the plays of a major American playwright:

Bonus Photo Question:
A scene from the 1952 movie version of a play by Carson McCullers. Name the movie and the three players shown here.

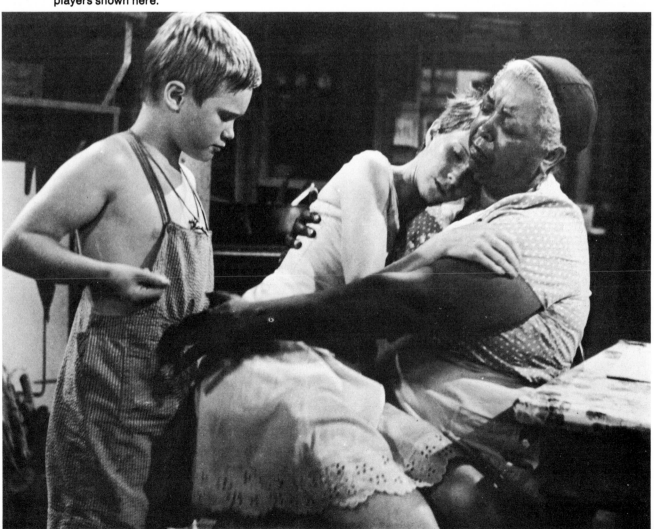

Bette Davis, Dean Martin, Shirley MacLaine, Sylvia Sidney. Name the playwright and the dramas that were adapted for the screen.

9. Which of the following plays was *not* turned into a movie musical: a) *Ah, Wilderness!* b) *My Sister Eileen* c) *They Knew What They Wanted*, or d) *The Women*?

10. Rosalind Russell has appeared in many film adaptations of stage plays. In which movie adaptations did she play a) a Jewish mama b) a stage mama c) an overbearing, overfastidious wife, and d) a widow who travels with the preserved corpse of her late husband?

11. In the original stage version of this play in early 1940, the role of the heroine's kid sister was played by Gene Tierney. In the 1942 film version, the role was played by Joan Leslie. In both versions, the hulking young football star on the college campus was played by Don DeFore. Enough hints? Name the play and movie.

12. On screen, the roles played on stage by Danny Kaye, Macdonald Carey, and Bert Lytell were played, respectively, by Mischa Auer, Ray Milland, and Warner Baxter. Can you name the property?

13. Frank Sinatra and Gene Kelly made a number of enjoyable movies together. But which role do they have in common?

14. A stage star's most famous role was played on screen by Norma Shearer in 1934, and by Jennifer Jones in 1957. Name this star, the role, and the play and movie.

15. True or false? The operetta *The Desert Song* was filmed three times, in 1929, 1943, and 1953. The leading role of the dashing hero was played, respectively, by John Boles, Dennis Morgan, and Howard Keel.

16. In the 1931 stage production of Eugene O'Neill's *Mourning Becomes Electra*, the part of the adulterous mother was played by Alla Nazimova. Who played this part in the 1947 film version?

17. Alfred Lunt, Lynn Fontanne, and Noel Coward starred in the stage version. Fredric March, Miriam Hopkins, and Gary Cooper appeared in the film version.

(Answers on page 153)

Name the play and movie.

18. Which one of the following films, all adapted from plays, won the Academy Award as the best picture of its year: a) *A Streetcar Named Desire* b) *A Man For All Seasons* c) *The King and I*, or d) *The Little Foxes*?

19. Ruth Gordon, Shirley Booth, Carol Channing, and Barbra Streisand, all have one role in common. Name the role—and the plays and films in which this central role appeared.

20. True or false? All the following films were turned into stage musicals: *The World of Henry Orient, The Quiet Man, Pride and Prejudice, All About Eve.*

21. The role played by David Wayne in the original stage version of *Mister Roberts* in 1948 was played in the 1955 film version by a) James Cagney b) Jack Lemmon, or c) Ward Bond?

22. Name the stage actress whose roles were played on screen by Joan Crawford, Ginger Rogers, and Deborah Kerr. (Hint: on screen *she* appeared in a stage role originated by Laurette Taylor.)

23. Plays often undergo strange casting changes on their trip from stage to screen. The performers grouped together here played the same role, the first on the stage, the second on the screen. You are asked to name the play and movie in which the role figured: a) Robert Alda—Marlon Brando b) Lauren Bacall—Ingrid Bergman c) Vincent Price—Charles Boyer, and d) Betty Field—Betty Hutton.

24. The 1938 stage version of Rodgers and Hart's musical, *The Boys From Syracuse*, featured Eddie Albert, Jimmy Savo, Muriel Angelus, and Teddy Hart. Can you name at least three of the principal players in the 1940 movie version?

25. Which *two* of the following actors did not appear in any film version of Hecht and MacArthur's comedy-melodrama, *The Front Page*: Pat O'Brien, Ralph Bellamy, Jack Lemmon, Lee Tracy, Adolphe Menjou, Edmund Lowe, Edward Everett Horton?

MOVIES OF THE SIXTIES

Here is a group of questions concerning movies released during the frenetic and traumatic sixties:

1. Name at least two actors who played the President of the United States in sixties films.

2. What does each of the following groups of sixties movies have in common: a) *The Mark* (1961). *The Loved One* (1965). *Doctor Zhivago* (1965). b) *It's a Mad, Mad, Mad, Mad World* (1963). *Ship of Fools* (1965). *Guess Who's Coming to Dinner* (1967). c) *Days of Wine and Roses* (1963). *The Wheeler Dealers* (1963). *The Hallelujah Trail* (1965).

3. Name the sixties movies in which you will find Minnie Castevet, Dianna Scott, and Sylvia Barrett. Also name the actresses who played them.

4. Carol Lynley and Carroll Baker played in two versions of the life of Jean Harlow. But who played Harlow's *mother* in these movies?

5. Which one of these songs from sixties movies won an Academy Award: a) "A Spoonful of Sugar" from *Mary Poppins* b) "Call Me Irresponsible" from *Papa's Delicate Condition* or c) "My Favorite Things" from *The Sound of Music*?

6. In the sixties, leading but aging actresses descended to playing grotesques in horror melodrama. In each of the following cases, name the actress and the movie: a) Trapped in an elevator inside her home, she is tormented by a group of nasty hoods. b) Thoroughly bonkers, the lady keeps the fiancée of her dead son a prisoner in her home. c) A batty recluse, she is driven to the brink of madness by her nasty cousin.

Bonus Photo Question:
James Westerfield, Karl Malden, and Burt Lancaster in the 1962 film about a convict who became a noted ornithologist in prison. What was the movie?

7. One of the finest films of 1960 was British, and its leading characters were military men named Jock Sinclair and Basil Barrow. Name this film.

8. In a 1961 hit movie, Paul Newman proclaimed, "I'm the best there is—even if you beat me I'm still the best there is." Name the movie.

9. Name the actress who played the title role in each of the following movies of the sixties: a) *Lolita* (1962) b) *Lilith* (1964) c) *Cat Ballou* (1965) d) *Who's Afraid of Virginia Woolf?* (1966) e) *Inside Daisy Clover* (1966).

10. "Benjamin Braddock disrupts Robinson-Smith wedding, rushes off with bride." In which movie did this occur?

11. The following players ended up very dead in movies of the sixties. Name the movies in which they met their demise: a) Suzanne Pleshette b) Piper Laurie, and c) Samantha Eggar.

12. Each of the following evokes a musical of the sixties. How many can you name? a) "That three-foot-three bundle of dynamite." "Small World." Mazeppa. b) Judge Billboard Rawkins. "Old Devil Moon." Francis Ford Coppola. c) Chimney sweeps. "Feed the Birds." Ed Wynn. d) "Lonely Goatherd." Charmian Carr. Robert Wise. e) Kay Medford. "Sadie." Mr. Arnstein.

13. Who played Susan Hayward's nasty, possessive mother in *Where Love Has Gone* (1964)?

14. Sex in the movies of the sixties became more explicit, with even the major studios giving way to leers and titillation. In which movie did each of the following occur: a) Robert Morse introduces Walter Matthau to the techniques of infidelity. b) A group of husbands, including James Garner and Tony Randall, install Kim Novak in an apartment as a roving, pass-around mistress. c) Ray Walston, hoping to interest Dean Martin in his songs, offers him the services of his "wife" for the night, substituting the town whore (Kim Novak) for the real lady.

15. Who played a) *The Man Who Shot Liberty Valance* (Also, who played Liberty Valance?) b) the major who headed *The Dirty Dozen* c) *Major Dundee* d) Charlie of *Goodbye Charlie*, and e) *Cool Hand Luke*?

16. Name the sixties movies in which you will find Norman Bates, Raymond Shaw, and Buck Barrow. Also name the actors who played them.

17. James Cagney made his last movie in 1961, playing C. R. McNamara, heading a Coca-Cola company in West Berlin. Name the film—and also name the actress who played his wife.

18. For each year, name the actor who received the Oscar for his performance: 1963: Albert Finney in *Tom Jones*, Sidney Poitier in *Lilies of the Field*, Paul Newman in *Hud*. 1965: Rod Steiger in *The Pawnbroker*, Richard Burton in *The Spy Who Came in From the Cold*, Lee Marvin in *Cat Ballou*. 1967: Warren Beatty in *Bonnie and Clyde*, Rod Steiger in *In the Heat of the Night*, Spencer Tracy in *Guess Who's Coming to Dinner*

19. There were some surprising pieces of casting in sixties films. In which movie did a) Barbara Stanwyck play a lesbian madam b) Shirley Jones play a vengeful prostitute, and c) Beatrice Lillie play a lady actively engaged in white slavery?

20. Name the stars who instructed us in 1966, in *How to Steal a Million*. And the star who demonstrated, very ineptly, *How to Murder Your Wife* (1965). (But nobody showed us *How to Stuff a Wild Bikini*.)

(Answers on page 153)

HOLDING COURT:
The Courtroom Drama in the Movies

By James Winchester

A dagger is hurled from the back of a courtroom and lodges in the witness *chair*, just inches away from chorine Dolores Divine, the witness who sits in it. Another witness is actually gunned down just as he is being sworn in. His killer escapes onto the ledge of the courthouse building, is shot at, tumbles over backwards, and falls several stories to his just desserts in the street below.

This is not a true story, torn from the tabloids, but a 1932 melodrama called *The Trial of Vivienne Ware*. In this Fox movie, Vivienne Ware, played by ingénue Joan Bennett, is charged in the shooting death of her fiancé. The victim was a scoundrel and a philanderer and wore a niggardly growth of hair over his lip (an abbreviation of the luxuriant growth of the nineteenth century stage villain) so that it is plain that he deserved to die. Besides, from the first, he had been a distraction to the likeable Miss Ware, as well as an obstruction to worthy, sincere John Sutherland (Donald Cook), a disappointed suitor whose disappointment doesn't diminish the fervor with which he defends Miss Ware in court—Mr. Sutherland is also a lawyer.

Vivienne Ware is based on a novel which had already been turned into a radio serial, "in which form," according to a contemporary review of the movie in *Variety*, "it got nationwide publicity and buildup from the Hearst newspaper chain." This previous incarnation as a radio serial, its brief (fifty-five minutes) running time, and the full-throttle speed of William K. Howard's direction explain why *Vivienne Ware* feels like a compilation of highlights from a movie serial, crammed together for viewing in a single sitting. *Vivienne Ware*, remarkable but unoffending, also suggests the extreme measures writers and directors often take when they face the task of extracting the drama out of courtroom trials which may, in fact, be long, fitful, and tedious. Certainly, extreme reactions account for some of the excesses of this sub-genre and, possibly, for many of its pleasures.

If you watched the "Perry Mason" television series during its long run, with Raymond Burr as Erle Stanley Gardner's unerring defender of the falsely accused, you became thoroughly schooled in the clichés of the courtroom melodrama. Each week—almost unfailingly—there was a pile-up of suspects (under way minutes into the program, since anyone exposed to more than one episode knew the discovery of a corpse or other indications of crime were imminent); a passionate exchange

between a likely victim and a likely prime suspect; an over-confident, not entirely likable prosecutor; a persevering, not overly emotional attorney for the defense; and the last-minute revelation of the actual culprit. This revelation usually made the guilty party spring up from his seat in the courtroom (making him more easily visible) and cry out either a shrill denial (which left no doubt of his guilt), or a shrill denunciation of his victim (which might also contain a summary account of his motives for the crime).

Gardner, a California lawyer who began publishing his Perry Mason mysteries in 1933 and didn't let up until his pen had gleaned about eighty of them from his teeming brain, wasn't the progenitor of these conventions. *Vivienne Ware* appeared the year before the first Perry Mason, and even earlier there had been the second film version of Elmer Rice's courtroom drama, *On Trial* (1928) and a movie derived from Bayard Veiller's popular play, *The Trial of Mary Dugan* (1929), with Norma Shearer as another innocent girl accused of murder. Also as far back as 1926, a former *Chicago Tribune* reporter

THE TRIAL OF VIVIENNE WARE (1932). With Joan Bennett and Donald Cook

ROXIE HART (1942). With George Montgomery and Ginger Rogers

had a hit comedy on Broadway which had as its subject the murder trial of an ambitious chorus girl. The play was *Chicago*, by Maurine Watkins, and it stood on end the already familiar conventions of courtroom drama and the tabloid coverage that turned trials into sensations. More recently, *Chicago* was the basis of the Bob Fosse musical of the same name, but the exuberant material was used to make something heavy, sour, and didactic. A version more faithful to the original source appeared in 1942 as *Roxie Hart*, with Ginger Rogers as the gal on trial and Adolphe Menjou as her suave defender, Billy Flynn. An added fillip, probably decreed by the Production Code, is that the movie Roxie is innocent of murder. She agrees to take the rap for her milksop husband (George Chandler) because she is persuaded by advisors that no jury will hang a woman and that the publicity will do wonders for her show business career.

The truth can be an obstacle to a successful defense, but it is an obstacle which Roxie's amoral lawyer can clear gracefully. He simply takes *accepted* courtroom tactics to their outrageous logical conclusion. He composes for Roxie her account of what happened up to the moment she supposedly shot her assailant, then coaches her on how to read it. He gets her to achieve a crescendo effect in her sobbing, and orchestrates her delivery so that

40

her sobs coincide with his dramatic pauses. He manipulates the media, represented by Spring Byington as a sob sister named Mary Sunshine. When a new inmate, "Two-Gun Gertie," played by Mayo Methot, steals the attention of the press, Roxie pretends that she is pregnant—there's good copy in a jailed expectant mother who faces the noose. Even *Vivienne Ware*, in emulation of *Chicago*, has its rhapsodizing sob sister in Miss Fairweather (ZaSu Pitts), who enumerates for her radio listeners each item of the dress worn by the defendant and the female witnesses.

Roxie Hart is courtroom *farce*, and one could cite many thirties' comedies, such as *You Can't Take It With You* and *Mr. Deeds Goes to Town*, which are resolved in courtrooms filled with eccentric people out of order. Apparently a courtroom can lend itself easily to comedy, as the Chicago 7 demonstrated several years ago, but it may not be quite so easy to bring off courtroom *drama*. The clichés are so familiar that the courtroom drama risks becoming farce if it doesn't fail on the other side by exercising a restraint whose effect is dullness. (The 1959 British courtroom drama, *Libel*, with Dirk Bogarde, is an example of discretion to the point of tedium.) The problem of dramatizing what happens inside a courtroom should be no more insoluble than dramatizing any other of life's situations. However, the writer is required to basically confine the action to one set. And probably the most explicitly dramatic action has taken place before the film is underway or at its outset.

Though courts are convened for many reasons, the movie courtroom usually involves a crime of violence and a baffling mystery about the perpetrator of that crime. The full-fledged courtroom drama is likely to begin with the commission of a crime or the discovery of one. If the audience isn't told, it usually senses that the drama will have to be resolved in court. If the film doesn't begin very early in the courtroom, everything that happens primes the audience for a climax within its walls. The effective courtroom drama keeps its audience in a state of nervous expectancy until it confers the relief that properly comes when the cameras finally move into the courtroom.

On this ground *Madame X* should be excluded from consideration, since its courtroom scene is merely an important episode in the film. However, this scene is such a splendid example of some of the excesses of courtroom drama that the story must be broached. Besides, the lady just won't be killed off. Based on a 1910 French play, *Madame X* was first filmed in 1916 with Pauline Frederick and remade four times thereafter. The story is ripe corn: a woman kills the man who threatens to reveal that a highly successful lawyer is the illegitimate son she gave up for adoption years before. On trial for her life, she refuses to disclose her motive for the crime and, of course, she is defended by her own son, who doesn't know that she is his mother. Inevitably, he loses this hopeless case and his mother is sent to her grave, where,

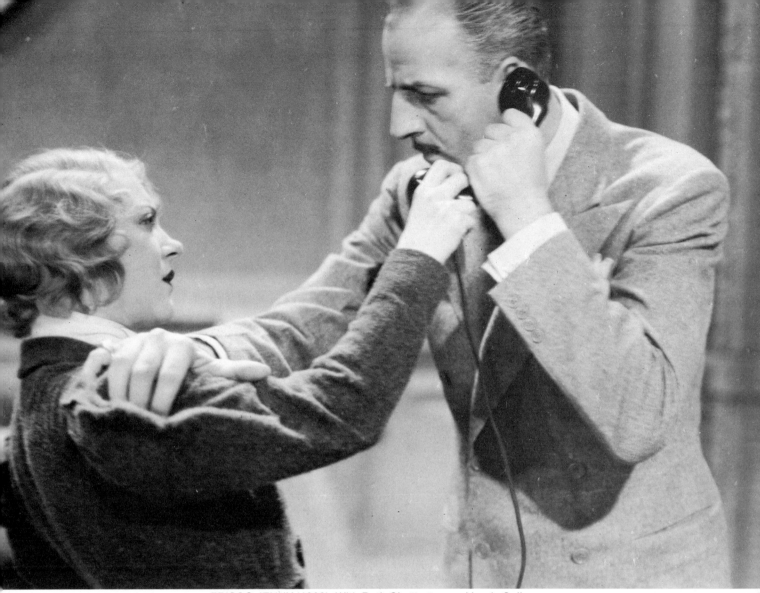

FRISCO JENNY (1933). With Ruth Chatterton and Louis Calhern

presumably, her secret is buried with her.

One would think that the outer limit of the courtroom drama had been reached with *Madame X*; however, Warner Bros., making unacknowledged use of the material in 1933, went one step further. Using Ruth Chatterton, the actress most associated with the Madame X role, the studio made *Frisco Jenny*. This film *begins* with the San Francisco earthquake, and winds up a few decades later with Jenny on trial for her life for killing the man who threatened to reveal that a highly successful district attorney is the illegitimate son she gave up for adoption years before. Again, she won't disclose her motive for the crime, but this time her own son, who doesn't know that she is his mother, *prosecutes* her, and wins a death sentence. The poor creature goes to her grave, taking the same sad secret with her. The casting doesn't make the D. A. any more sympathetic; he is played by the joyless Donald Cook, late of *The Trial of Vivienne Ware*. Perhaps the most preposterous thing about the film is that by her strength and enormous skill Ruth Chatterton

can give such a role dignity and make it work.

Courtroom dramas are rarely developed directly for the screen. Clifford Odets wrote an original screenplay for *The Story on Page One* (1960), with Rita Hayworth and Gig Young as lovers on trial for murdering her husband. (Odets directed it himself.) But more often the courtroom drama has evolved from material developed for another medium: a teleplay, as was the case with *Judgment at Nuremberg* (1961); a novel, *The Paradine Case* (1948) or *Trial* (1955); a stage play, *The Winslow Boy* (1950); or both a novel and play, *The Caine Mutiny* (1954). Often, the film is based on a real-life case that gained notoriety, as with *Compulsion* (1959), which was a thinly disguised version of the Leopold-Loeb case of the twenties; *Inherit the Wind* (1960), which was based on the Scopes "Monkey" trial of the same period; and *The Lawyer* (1970), which bore a resemblance to the 1954 Sam Sheppard murder trial. (Several years later, *The Lawyer* and its star, Barry Newman, were reactivated for the television series, "Petrocelli.")

THE PARADINE CASE (1948). A trial at the Old Bailey in England

As much as it is a test for writers and directors, the courtroom drama can also be an actor's opportunity. Lionel Barrymore as an alcoholic lawyer in *A Free Soul* (1931), Maximilian Schell as the defense attorney in *Judgment at Nuremberg* (1961), and Gregory Peck as a high-minded Southern lawyer in *To Kill a Mockingbird* (1962) received Oscars for their performances in the courtroom, and Paul Muni is probably best remembered as Emile Zola defending Alfred Dreyfus in the courtroom climax of *The Life of Emile Zola* (1937). One of the great hammy performances is Charles Laughton's in that model of courtroom entertainments, *Witness for the Prosecution*. As Sir Wilfrid Robarts, the artful, ailing barrister who defends an accused murderer (Tyrone Power) while being plagued by an over-solicitous nurse (Elsa Lanchester), Laughton is richly comic.

Witness for the Prosecution is a movie with not a thing

on its mind except drawing the audience into its make-believe world of English jurisprudence and keeping it alert. Before Billy Wilder directed the film in 1957, it had already been a hit play by Agatha Christie on Broadway and in London. A couple of decades before that, it had been a short story with a surprise ending, also by Christie. In the complex but devilishly clever plot line, Laughton is coaxed out of retirement by the prospect of obtaining the acquittal of a charming man accused of murdering a rich widow for her money. The case is complicated by the ambiguous behavior and motives of the accused's wife (Marlene Dietrich). Much as Alfred Hitchcock, in *Psycho* (1960), had exploited an audience's assumption about the inviolability of the putative star and main character, Agatha Christie tricks her audience by exploiting British xenophobia. Audiences accept the worst about the wife of the accused because she is a foreigner—a German whom

WITNESS FOR THE PROSECUTION (1958). Marlene
Dietrich as Christine Vole

he had loved and, by marrying, rescued from wartime Germany. The famous surprise endings are so stunning that audiences are diverted from thinking too seriously about their credibility.

Another successful courtroom melodrama from the same period seems almost like the sleazy obverse of *Witness for the Prosecution*. In Otto Preminger's 1959 film, *Anatomy of a Murder*, the engagingly squalid subject matter is the murder trial of a man who has killed his wife's alleged rapist. His innocence is predicated upon two things: the determination that his wife was, in fact, raped, and the credibility of his claim that he acted upon an "irresistible impulse," an obscure and infrequently cited defense that his lawyer digs up. The film was based on a best-selling novel by Robert Traver, actually John Voelker, a Michigan Supreme Court justice who had defended an Army lieutenant and gained his acquittal for

the fatal shooting of a tavern owner in Big Bay, Michigan in 1951. (When the movie appeared, the victim's widow filed suit against Voelker, but the case was eventually dismissed.) Preminger had made a courtroom drama before, *The Court-Martial of Billy Mitchell* (1955), but this time he broke away from the studio to shoot the film entirely on location. Voelker's own frequent residence and law office served as the unkempt bachelor quarters of his fictional counterpart, Paul Biegler, played by James Stewart. The fresh locations of Michigan's Upper Peninsula, shot in almost documentary style black-and-white, provided a stark backdrop for the drama, and gave the film an authentic feel.

The casting of the principal roles was also first rate. James Stewart plays the lawyer sympathetic to his young client and his wife. Arthur O'Connell is his boozing sidekick, who helps with the case. Ben Gazzara has a dry

ANATOMY OF A MURDER (1959). With George C. Scott, Joseph N. Welch, and Ben Gazzara

iciness as the inscrutable lieutenant. The role of the sexy wife fell to Lee Remick after Lana Turner's withdrawal from the film because Preminger refused to upgrade her wardrobe to one Miss Turner thought befitting her glamour girl image. George C. Scott played the prosecutor, and, in the shrewdest bit of casting, Joseph N. Welch, the attorney who had gained national recognition during the Army-McCarthy hearings, played a wry, humane, and eloquent judge much like himself.

Recently, television has been dramatizing many important cases—the Chicago 7, Charles Manson—and resurrecting some older ones on which doubt is cast about the judgment that was handed down—the trials of the Scottsboro Boys and the Rosenbergs. (The Lindbergh kidnapping case was also recreated.) No doubt audiences can look forward, on television and in the movies, to dramatizations of the Patty Hearst trial. And several months ago, Peter Reilly, the young man convicted of manslaughter in the killing of his mother, won an appeal for a new trial after his case gained national attention through the work of playwright Arthur Miller and *The New York Times*. The following week, Reilly announced that he had signed over publishing and movie rights to a former *Time/Life* correspondent.

No doubt as long as audiences continue to enjoy the intricacies of courtroom procedures and the dramatic clashes over guilt or innocence, movie theaters will continue to ring with the sound of the gavel and cry of "Order in the court!"

THE SPIRIT OF ADVENTURE

Off we go to the never-never world of derring-do! This quiz concerns the perennially popular genre of the adventure film, featuring intrepid heroes and dashing swashbucklers (or is it swashing dashbucklers?), demure heroines, and dastardly villains.

1. One of the screen's most glorious adventure movies was Warners' *The Adventures of Robin Hood* (1938). Most moviegoers recall Robin and his Merrie Men. But which *three* of the following actors played the villains: Melville Cooper, Basil Rathbone, Henry Daniell, Vincent Price, Claude Rains, Bruce Cabot?

2. Name the Technicolor movie in which Sabu played Abu, the Little Thief, who proclaims, "Everything is possible when seen through the eyes of youth!"

3. Who played the wan heroine in the classic adventure film, *Gunga Din* (1939)?

4. A popular 1950 film was a remake of a 1937 film which starred Cedric Hardwicke as adventurous Allan Quartermain. Name the film.

5. William Wellman's war drama, *Wings* (1927), featured a brief performance by a young actor who appears as an ace pilot with the credo, "Luck or no luck, when your time comes, you're going to get it." Minutes later, he "gets it." His name?

Bonus Photo Question:
Paulette Goddard is trapped by the Indians in this 1947 adventure movie from Cecil B. DeMille. Name the movie, and also name the actor playing the solemn, tattooed Indian chieftain at Miss Goddard's right.

6. A standard gambit of swashbuckling movies was the hero disguised as a foppish, effete member of the opposition. Can you provide the more colorful and adventurous movie names for Sir Percy Blakeney and for Diego?

7. *The Four Feathers*, filmed in 1921, 1928, and 1939, was a stirring tale of heroism and cowardice among British soldiers fighting in Sudan. It was remade in 1956 as a) *East of Sudan* b) *Soldiers Three*, or c) *Storm Over the Nile*?

8. In which movie did Claudette Colbert play a French-accented camp follower named Cigarette, who gives her life to save her beloved Legionnaire?

9. This Technicolor drama, concerning an expedition by Rogers' Rangers into dangerous Indian territory, included a talked-about scene in which a crazed ranger insists on keeping the head of one of his Indian victims. Name the movie.

10. Which of the following actors *never* portrayed frontier gunman Wild Bill Hickok in films: Richard Dix, Howard Keel, Don Murray, Dana Andrews, Jeff Corey?

11. In the 1932 African adventure, *Red Dust*, the hero was played by Clark Gable. Who played the role in the 1953 remake?

12. Howard Hawks' *Only Angels Have Wings* (1939) featured a former silent-film star who hadn't made a movie in four years. (Probably his best-known film: *Tol'able David*, 1922) His name?

13. In which movie did Errol Flynn play pirate captain Geoffrey Thorpe, leading his buccaneers against the Spanish fleet?

14. Warners' *The Charge of the Light Brigade* (1936) was a large-scale adventure that celebrated the rash bravery of the "six hundred" who marched into "the Valley of Death." Ironically, the British remake in 1968 stressed the stupidity and brutality of the military mind. Name at least two of the stars of the 1968 version.

15. In the 1937 and 1952 versions of *The Prisoner of Zenda*, who played the arch-villain Rupert of Hentzau?

16. Name the role played by Ronald Colman, Gary Cooper, and Guy Stockwell in three film versions of the same story. (The title is the role.)

17. The following actors all played the central role in various movie versions of a famous adventure tale: Douglas Fairbanks, Walter Abel, Don Ameche, and Gene Kelly. Name the tale—and the role.

18. Who played the role of Captain Bligh in the 1962 remake of *Mutiny on the Bounty*: a) Robert Shaw b) Trevor Howard c) Richard Harris, or d) James Mason?

19. This dramatic war story was filmed twice, with the following actors in the same leading roles: Richard Barthelmess and Errol Flynn; Douglas Fairbanks, Jr. and David Niven; Neil Hamilton and Basil Rathbone. What was this story?

20. A 1950 movie from Warners, entitled *The Flame and the Arrow*, used old *Robin Hood* sets for its tale of a swashbuckling hero named Dardo the Arrow. This time, however, the star wasn't Errol Flynn but a) Kirk Douglas b) Burt Lancaster c) Alan Ladd, or d) Dennis Morgan?

(Answers on page 154)

RIGHT ON, LADIES!

Hollywood movies have not been known to expound the feminist point of view. In fact, most films have given short shrift to women, confining them largely to roles as either wide-eyed heroines and sacrificing mothers or vamps and vixens no better than they should be.

Occasionally, however, women have appeared as strong-minded characters, bent on pursuing their own careers and/or inclinations. And if most of them ended up in the hero's arms, they at least had their day in the sun.

Here is a group of these independent ladies. How many can you identify? Who played the roles—and in which films?

1. Dottie Peale, powerful magazine publisher who becomes romantically involved with an army general.

2. Dr. Emily Barringer, the first woman to serve on the staff of a municipal hospital in New York City.

3. Dr. Constance Petersen, a psychiatrist who becomes involved in the life of a possibly homicidal amnesia victim.

4. Amanda Farrow, nasty, employee-baiting executive of Fabian Publications.

5. Linda Gilman, glamorous but business-like editor of *Home Life* Magazine

6. Kay Thorndyke, high-pressure publisher who influences Grant Matthews to run for the Presidential nomination.

7. Susan Middlecott, dean of a New England woman's college, who has a romance with an English astronomy professor.

8. Julia Treadway, powerful daughter of the founder of a huge corporation—and mistress of the just-deceased head of that corporation.

9. Clarissa Standish, mayor of a small Maine town, who meets—and has a rocky relationship with—another mayor at a San Francisco convention.

10. Liza Elliott, a domineering but troubled fashion magazine editor.

11. Helen Brown, a research psychologist who becomes romantically entangled with a scandal-magazine writer.

12. Anne Crandall, a widowed small-town mayor who commissions amorous sculptor George Corday to create a new statue of her late husband.

13. Amanda Bonner, lawyer and active competitor to her lawyer husband Adam.

14. Phoebe Snow, Congresswoman from Iowa, sent with a committee to investigate the morale of American troops in Berlin.

15. Julia Winslow Garth, a Boston doctor who arrives in Sante Fe in 1880 and proceeds to set things right. (She also marries the town's leading doctor.)

(Answers on page 154)

Bonus Photo Question:
In this 1945 movie, Irene Dunne played a famous writer who follows her husband when he reports to officer's candidate school. She shares this scene with husband Alexander Knox and publisher Charles Coburn. The movie's name?

47

"AND THE WINNER IS . . ."

As an adjunct to Jeanine Basinger's article on Oscar, here are twenty memory-stretching questions about winners of the Academy Awards over the years.

1. Which of the following actors never received an Academy Award nomination for Best Actor: Maurice Chevalier, Wallace Beery, John Garfield, or Mickey Rooney?

2. The Oscar for the Best Picture in 1935 went to which of these movies: a) *The Informer* b) *David Copperfield*, or c) *Mutiny on the Bounty*?

3. Can you name the three movies for which Walter Brennan won his three Oscars as Best Supporting Actor?

4. Director George Cukor has received only one Oscar over the years—for which of these films: a) *Little Women* b) *Camille* c) *A Star is Born* (1937), or d) *My Fair Lady*?

5. *The Graduate* (1967) received nominations in the major categories of Best Film, Best Actor, Best Actress, and Best Director. In which one category did it win?

6. Which of these songs won the Academy Award as the best song of 1956: a) "Around the World" b) "Hello, Young Lovers," or c) "Que Sera, Sera?"

7. Name the only two actresses to win the Best Actress Award two years in succession—and the films for which they won the awards.

8. The Foreign Language Film Award for 1972 was given to a) *Cries and Whispers* b) *The Emigrants*, or c) *The Discreet Charm of the Bourgeoisie*?

9. The first Academy Award for Best Performance by an Actor was won by a) Charles Chaplin b) Emil Jannings c) Walter Huston, or d) Richard Barthelmess?

10. Since 1937 (though not every year), the Academy of Motion Picture Arts and Sciences has presented the Irving G. Thalberg Memorial Award to a distinguished member of the film world, as a tribute to the late MGM producer. Who won the first Thalberg Award in 1937: a) Louis B. Mayer b) Darryl F. Zanuck, or c) Hal B. Wallis?

11. In 1967, the Oscar for the Best Original Screenplay was given to a) *Bonnie and Clyde* b) *The Emigrants*, or c) *Guess Who's Coming To Dinner*?

12. In 1939, all but one of the major Academy Awards (Picture, Actor, Actress, Director, Supporting Actor, Supporting Actress) were won by *Gone With the Wind*. Which award did *not* go to the film?

13. In 1940, Bette Davis was nominated for her performance in *The Letter*. A dozen years earlier, an actress was nominated for the same role. Who was she?

14. *Citizen Kane* (1941) is generally regarded as one of the greatest films ever made. Yet it won an Academy Award in only one category. Was this a) Best Cinematography—Black and White b) Best Music Score of a Dramatic Picture, or c) Best Original Screenplay?

15. Twenty-three years after winning an Academy Award for *The Story of Louis Pasteur*, Paul Muni was nominated as Best Actor for his performance in which movie?

16. John Wayne won his first Academy Award as Best Actor in 1969 for his performance as Rooster Cogburn in *True Grit*. He had been nominated only once before, for his performance in which of these films: a) *Red River* b) *Sands of Iwo Jima*, or c) *The High and the Mighty*?

17. From the following list of actresses, select those who won Academy Awards for their very first performances in films: Jennifer Jones, Eva Marie Saint, Audrey Hepburn, Sandy Dennis, Barbra Streisand.

18. Which of the following foreign-born actresses never won an Academy Award: Anna Magnani, Liv Ullmann, Simone Signoret, Sophia Loren?

19. In 1970 Helen Hayes was named Best Supporting Actress for her performance in *Airport*. Nearly four decades earlier, she had received Best Actress award for her performance in which of these movies: a) *The Sin of Madelon Claudet* b) *A Farewell to Arms*, or c) *The White Sister*?

20. A tough cop and a tough call girl won the Best Actor/Best Actress Awards in 1971. Name the performers who played these roles, and the films in which they appeared.

(Answers on page 154)

Bonus Photo Question:
The famous beach scene from FROM HERE TO ETERNITY (1953), with Burt Lancaster and Deborah Kerr. The movie won the Academy Award as Best Picture, but were these two stars nominated for Oscars? And did they win?

49

THE SPORTING LIFE

Movies about sports have not always been popular with the public, but many of them were solidly made films that have survived the years. Here is a group of questions about sports movies—and performers who played sports figures.

1. Name the sport involved in each of the following movies: a) *Rhubarb* b) *Hard, Fast and Beautiful*, and c) *Number One*.

2. Name the movies in which Clark Gable, Paul Newman, and Steve McQueen play racing drivers.

3. Horse racing has been a frequent movie subject over the years. Name the racing movie in which a) Richard Greene and Loretta Young are on opposite sides of a feud about horses. b) John Payne defies mother Fay Bainter and rides a prize horse to victory. c) Elizabeth Taylor and Mickey Rooney train their beloved horse for a championship race.

4. Which of the following actors never played a bullfighter: a) Tyrone Power b) Robert Evans c) Cornel Wilde, or d) Robert Stack?

5. "PAT PEMBERTON OPPOSES BABE DIDRIKSON ZAHARIAS IN GOLF MATCH!" Name the movie in which this headline might have appeared. And who played Pat and Babe?

6. Our inventive academics: Professor Ray Milland discovers a serum which, when applied to a baseball, makes the ball completely repulsive to wood. Professor Fred MacMurray discovers a substance which, applied to the shoes of a basketball player, causes the player to leap into the air. Name the two films in which these goings-on go on.

7. In which movie did Edward G. Robinson train the New York Giants? And in which movie did Paul Douglas manage the Pittsburgh Pirates?

8. *The Crowd Roars* (1932), a movie about car racing, was remade by Warner Bros. as a) *Racing Blood* b) *Fast Company*, or c) *Indianapolis Speedway*?

9. In 1950, Fox filmed Ernest Hemingway's story, "My Old Man," about a jockey and his son, under the title a) *Boots Malone* b) *Under My Skin*, or c) *The Homestretch*?

10. Name the performer who played each of the following sports figures and the film in which he/she played the role: a) Ben Hogan b) Annette Kellerman, and c) Grover Cleveland Alexander.

11. The poignant story of Jimmy Piersall, the young baseball star who had a mental breakdown, was filmed in 1957 as *Fear Strikes Out*, with Anthony Perkins. Who played his domineering father: a) Ed Begley b) Karl Malden, or c) Arthur Kennedy?

12. Name the films in which Greta Garbo and Marlon Brando played ski instructors.

13. Boxers seem to have special problems among movie sportsmen. Joe Bonaparte really wanted to play the violin. Danny Kenny had to support a musician brother. And Paul Callan was a deaf mute! Name the actors who played these roles—and the films in which they appeared.

14. How do you win a baseball pennant? With "heart," of course. Name the film in which this was demonstrated. (Hint: it also takes "a little brains, a little talent.")

15. In *Designing Woman* (1957), a very funny performance as a punch-drunk fighter who sleeps with his eyes open was given by a) Mickey Shaughnessy b) Aldo Ray, or c) William Bendix?

16. A well-remembered moment in *Knute Rockne—All American* has player George Gipp, on his death-bed, tell Pat O'Brien as coach Rockne, "Some day, when things are tough, maybe you can ask the boys to go in there and win just once for the Gipper." Who played the Gipper?

17. Name the actor who played a boxer in each of the following movies: a) *Fat City* b) *Body and Soul*, and c) *The Set-Up*.

18. Big-game hunting is a sport to many, a cruel indulgence to many others. But it often makes for exciting action on the screen. Name the "big-game" movie in which a) John Wayne traps animals and sells them to zoos around the world b) Trevor Howard is obsessed with saving the elephants from man's aggression, and c) Stewart Granger is a hunter obsessed with catching a predatory tiger.

19. In *Pride of the Yankees*, the story of ballplayer Lou Gehrig, who played the role of famed ballplayer Babe Ruth?

20. One of the best moments in films about sports has ballplayer James Stewart trying out his wooden leg for the first time, gamely clutching the hand of his tiny son. Name the movie in which this moment occurs.

(Answers on page 154)

PHANTOMS OF THE MOVIES STRIKE AGAIN

By Ted Sennett

In the first *Movie Buff's Book*, Curtis F. Brown offered a list of movies designed to cure what he called "a galloping case of *Rerepeatitis televisionus*," or simple weariness at seeing the same old movies on television for the umpteenth time. He called them "Movies That Might Have Been (and probably Just As Well Weren't)," and he described them in the typical style of your favorite television guide.

By some strange fluke, we have just uncovered a fresh batch of these films. Again, you will not find them on any television screen, not even in the middle of the night. Most likely, you will have to resort to another showing of *Casablanca* or *The Maltese Falcon*. (Pity.) But they should remind you of days of yore, when Really Rotten Movies were yours for a mere pittance.

7:30 (9) *She Wouldn't Say Maybe* (1940). Small-town soda jerk meets runaway princess disguised as a canner in a herring factory. Richard Crane, Sheila Ryan, Leonid Kinskey, Adeline De Walt Reynolds.

9:15 (2) *Jungle Rot* (1942). Mysterious woman named Holdamayo lures fever-ridden archaeologist into remote Amazon swamp. Sigrid Gurie, Grady Sutton, Mantan Moreland, Victor Kilian.

11:30 (2) *Live, Darn Ya, Live!* (1937). Siamese dancing act forced to split when one gets offer for Palace. Unusual musical. Dixie Dunbar, Ella Logan, James Dunn, the Nicholas Brothers.

8:00 (3) *Bar None* (1941). Experimental prison on honor system is hit by a wave of homicides and naughty behavior. George Reeves, Barton MacLane, Albert Dekker, Eduardo Ciannelli.

9:00 (12) *Hold the Headlines* (1936). Comedy-mystery. Two reporters in love fight to scoop a sensational story on sewage disposal in the big town. James Dunn, Marian Marsh, Eddie Quillan, Dennie Moore.

12:00 (5) *Kiss Me, Nauseous* (1947). *Film-noir* melodrama. Private eye loses blonde suspect, catches bad head cold, in rain-swept streets of Frisco. Dick Powell, William Bendix, Mona Maris, Butterfly McQueen.

3:00 (9) *Close Shave for Dr. Kildare* (1943). Complications at Blair Hospital, centering on Dr. Kildare's emergency hernia operation—and Dr. Gillespie's infected hickey from Nurse Byrd. Lew Ayres, Lionel Barrymore, Alma Kruger, Nat Pendleton.

11:30 (7) *Five Dads for Murgatroyd* (1938). Five middle-aged bachelors adopt orphan who grows up to have them committed to an asylum. Baby Sandy, William Demarest, Mischa Auer, Chester Clute.

2:30 (11) *Fly Towards Tomorrow* (1942). Courageous pilot, blinded in accident, insists on continuing to fly cross-country passenger plane. Lee Bowman, Ann Richards, Cecil Kellaway, Paul Kelly.

10:00 (9) *Sahara Wildcat* (1940). Desert chieftain comes upon sultan's daughter suffering from severe case of windburn. Jon Hall, Evelyn Ankers, Douglass Dumbrille, Joan Davis.

8:00 (3) *A Pox On Miss Prewitt* (1943). A group of Miss Amanda Prewitt's students over fifty years reminisce about the nasty old sadist. Hope Emerson, Elisha Cook, Jr., Rondo Hatton, Jack Elam.

4:30 (2) *Westward, the Greyhound* (1944). Sheep herders and homesteaders join forces to halt inroads of charter bus company and Hilton hotel chain. Broderick Crawford, Binnie Barnes, Chill Wills, Marie Windsor.

7:00 (4) *April in Tijuana* (1941). Color musical. Taxi driver and dog race entrepreneur vie for affections of tortilla stuffer. Cesar Romero, Carmen Miranda, Dick Haymes, Billy Gilbert.

11:00 (7) *Ladies Never Listen* (1934). Married society leader dallies with croupier, jewel thief, gigolo, and French baron. Ann Harding, Gilbert Roland, Paul Lukas, Edmund Lowe, Alexander D'Arcy.

9:30 (5) *Skip to Mai Lu* (1940). Exotic melodrama. Girl known as Taiwan Tessie hides soggy military secrets in bowl of won-ton soup. Anna May Wong, Edna May Oliver, Keye Luke, Gregory Ratoff.

6:30 (9) *Next Stop: Stillwell Avenue* (1942). Danger and suspense on the Sea Beach Express in Brooklyn—who poisoned the box of Good 'n' Plenty? Louise Allbritton, Steven Geray, Richard

Lane, Barbara Pepper.

12:30 (11) *Shame on Sylvia* (1932). Small-town girl gets involved with gangster, starts selling ice cream with illegally low amount of butter fat. Constance Bennett, Alan Dinehart, Eric Linden, Clara Blandick.

2:00 (3) *Sherlock Holmes Faces Mecca* (1943). Newly uncovered Holmes adventure has detective tracing jewel-studded burnoose to Afghanistan. Edward Everett Horton, Eric Blore, Heather Angel, Melville Cooper.

8:45 (12) *Evil Weevil* (1939). In the heart of the southland, a blood-thirsty vampire named Bela Cotten threatens the lives of the plantation damsels. Monty Woolley, Marjorie Weaver, Gil Lamb.

3:15 (2) *Eighty Words a Minute* (1933). Trouble-shooting clerk-typists take a dip in the steno pool. Stuart Erwin, Jack Oakie, Mary Carlisle, Etienne Girardot.

Marian Marsh and James Dunn in a scene from HOLD THE HEADLINES (1936), a.k.a. COME CLOSER, FOLKS

PAUSE FOR A
MUSICAL NUMBER

Here's a new musical quiz. Simply match the song at the left with the non-musical movie in which it appeared, either as a featured tune or as the principal musical theme:

"Oh, Give Me Time for Tenderness" *A Night at the Opera*
"Rock Around the Clock" *A Foreign Affair*
"Moon River" *Stage Fright*
"See What the Boys in the Back Room Will Have" *A Guy Named Joe*
"Cosi-Cosa" *Dark Victory*
"The Sounds of Silence" *Saratoga Trunk*
"The Sweetheart Tree" *Inside Daisy Clover*
"I'll Get By" *The Razor's Edge*
"High Hopes" *Destry Rides Again*
"Moon of Manakoora" *The Blackboard Jungle*
"Illusions" *Now, Voyager*
"Mam'selle" *Breakfast at Tiffany's*
"The Shadow of Your Smile" *Gilda*
"As Long As I Live" *The Great Race*
"The Laziest Gal in Town" *Arch of Triumph*
"I'm Writing a Letter to Daddy" *The Graduate*
"You're Gonna Hear From Me" *The Sandpiper*
"Long After Tonight" *The Hurricane*
"Put the Blame on Mame" *What Ever Happened to Baby Jane?*
"It Can't Be Wrong" *A Hole in the Head*

(Answers on page 155)

Bonus Photo Question:
In Alfred Hitchcock's THE MAN WHO KNEW TOO MUCH (1956), James Stewart comforts Doris Day, distraught at the kidnapping of their son. Name the song that appeared in this movie as a key factor in the resolution.

ONE GOOD MOVIE (SOMETIMES) DESERVES ANOTHER

In movies (and elsewhere), success induces the urge to repeat or duplicate that success. Here is a group of questions about movies that inspired other movies, either sequels or an entire series. (Occasionally, the enthusiasm wasn't justified.)

1. Name the actress who played opposite Bob Hope in each of the following: a) *My Favorite Blonde* b) *My Favorite Brunette* and c) *My Favorite Spy*.

2. The first Hardy family movie was called a) *Love Finds Andy Hardy* b) *A Family Affair*, or c) *Judge Hardy and Son*?

3. In *Father of the Bride* (1950) and the sequel, *Father's Little Dividend* (1951), who played Mother?

4. Which one of the following actors never dallied with Maisie (Ann Sothern), MGM's heart-of-gold showgirl of the forties: a) George Murphy b) Red Skelton, or c) Van Johnson?

5. A character played by Alan Ladd in *The Carpetbaggers* (1964) "inspired" a later movie with Steve McQueen called a) *Nevada Smith* b) *Joe Dakota*, or c) *Montana Mike*?

6. True or false? Claude Rains played Jack Griffin, *The Invisible Man*, only once.

7. *Four Daughters* (1938), Warners' popular soap opera from Fannie Hurst's story, produced several sequels. Name the actresses who played the four Lemp girls.

8. The sequel to the successful *Cheaper by the Dozen* (1950) was called a) *Bachelor's Daughters* b) *Yours, Mine, and Ours* or c) *Belles On Their Toes*?

9. After Lynn Belvedere, that snobbish, know-it-all jack-of-all trades, solved everyone's problems in *Sitting Pretty* (1948), he went on to college and a home for the elderly. Name the movie in which he worked his magic on the old folks.

10. Which was the first James Bond adventure: a) *From Russia With Love* b) *Dr. No*, or c) *Goldfinger*?

11. Which of the following actors never played Tarzan in the movies: Lex Barker, Gordon Scott, Steve Reeves, or Jock Mahoney?

12. Name the actress who played the title role in each of the following: a) *Dear Ruth* (1947) b) *Dear Wife* (1949) and c) *Dear Brat* (1951).

13. In the following list of players are the names of the two who played the parents of Nick Charles, the wrongly named "Thin Man," in *The Thin Man Goes Home* (1944), the fifth movie of the popular mystery series: Harry Davenport, Fay Holden, Beulah Bondi, Charles Coburn, Lucile Watson, Samuel S. Hinds. Name these two players.

14. The success of *On Moonlight Bay* (1951), Warners' period musical starring Doris Day, prompted the studio to make another musical involving the same family. It was called a) *Shine On, Harvest Moon* b) *By the Light of the Silvery Moon*, or c) *Moonlight in Vermont*?

15. The popularity of Sidney Poitier in the role of Police Lieutenant Virgil Tibbs in *In the Heat of the Night* (1967) led to two more movies with the same character: *They Call Me Mr. Tibbs* and a) *The Organization* b) *The Lost Man* or c) *The Split*?

16. *Ensign Pulver* (1964) was a poor sequel to the acclaimed *Mister Roberts*, picking up the character of the raffish, resourceful Pulver played by Jack Lemmon in the original movie. Who played Pulver in the sequel: a) Nick Adams b) Tony Curtis, or c) Robert Walker, Jr.?

17. One of the following titles for the long-running Henry Aldrich series is a phony: a) *Henry Aldrich Swings It* b) *Henry Aldrich, Detective*, and c) *Henry Aldrich Gets Glamour*. Which is the phony?

18. The movies' first Dr. Kildare was played by a) Joel McCrea b) Lew Ayres, or c) Robert Young?

19. There were two sequels to *Topper* (1937): *Topper Takes a Trip* (1939) and *Topper Returns* (1941). In which of these films did Cary Grant appear in his original role of George Kirby?

20. All but one of the following actresses appeared in Columbia's "Blondie" series: Janet Blair, Rita Hayworth, Anita Louise, Marguerite Chapman. Name the one who never made it.

(Answers on page 155)

CUT THAT OUT!

In the first *Movie Buff's Book*, we presented a number of rare photographs showing footage that had been excised from films for a variety of reasons. Sometimes the star had to be replaced; other times the movie ran too long. Occasionally, an entire scene was removed to keep the action flowing more smoothly.

Here are more photographs of movie moments that never made it to the theaters.

In Darryl F. Zanuck's 1939 production of *Drums Along the Mohawk*, the small role of Mary Reall was originally cast with young Linda Darnell. Zanuck pulled her out to co-star with Tyrone Power in *Day-Time Wife*, and Dorris Bowdon took over the role. Here's Linda Darnell in a never-seen scene with Robert Lowery.

A deleted scene from *The Man Who Came to Dinner* (1941), with Laura Hope Crews, Monty Woolley, and Bette Davis. Miss Crews never appeared in the movie.

Tommy Nolan and Peter Sellers in a scene from Billy Wilder's *Kiss Me, Stupid* (1964), shot before Sellers' heart attack forced his replacement by Ray Walston.

Marlene Dietrich and Glynis Johns in deleted footage from *No Highway in the Sky* (1951).

An excised scene from Twentieth Century-Fox's production of Ernest Hemingway's *The Snows of Kilimanjaro* (1952), showing Hildegarde Neff as the character named Countess Liz as she renders a tune for a motley group of socialites on the Riviera.

In the 1962 film version of *Gypsy*, Natalie Wood, Rosalind Russell, and Karl Malden performed the Jule Styne-Stephen Sondheim song "Together." It was later cut from the release print of the movie.

In the 1964 melodrama, *Lady in a Cage*, Olivia de Havilland played a rich woman imprisoned and tormented by a vicious trio of teenagers. She finally escapes, and the movie as originally shot had her re-united with her son, William Swan. The released movie retained the happy ending but this reunion scene was cut.

In 1959, during the filming of *Solomon and Sheba*, Tyrone Power collapsed and died of a heart attack. He was replaced by Yul Brynner. Here is Power in a scene with George Sanders. In the background: Marisa Pavan.

Another scene from the original, scuttled version of *Solomon and Sheba* with Tyrone Power.

This courtroom scene from the 1962 version of Lillian Hellman's *The Children's Hour*, co-starring Shirley MacLaine and Audrey Hepburn, was never seen in the released film.

In this scene from *Ship of Fools* (1965), Vivien Leigh and Christiane Schmidtmer prepare for bed on their ocean voyage. The scene never appeared in the released film.

Lidia Prochnicka and Candice Bergen in a scene removed from the release print of *The Group* (1966).

A CROSSWORD PUZZLE
FOR MOVIE BUFFS
By Curtis F. Brown

ACROSS

1 Part of 1954 Oscar-winning song
8 *Make Me a——*
12 British-American actress (*The Blue Danube, The Purple Mask, Blue Hawaii*)
13 Fritz Lang's scriptwriter wife von Harbou
14 First name of Danish-born actress (*Honeymoon in Bali, Tokyo Rose*)
15 Ingrid's newscaster daughter
16 Danish-born director (*Hitler's Madman, Written on the Wind*)
17 Exclamations of disbelief (2 wds.)
20 College campus political org. of sixties
22 "They put their Scotch or —— down and lie down . . ." (Noël Coward song "Mad Dogs and Englishmen")
23 Salesman's territory (abbr.)
25 "—— and sandals," insider's term for Biblical epic
27 *Black ——*, with Karloff
31 British character actor (*Lorna Doone, Rembrandt, Jamaica Inn, I Know Where I'm Going*)
34 Eddie went to town as him
35 It afforded Pat and Mel Oscars
37 Gloria's nickname in *Oklahoma!*
38 Eldest Gabor sister
41 Belonging to Broadway-Hollywood writer (*Bachelor Mother, Indiscreet, Let's Make Love*)
44 Other half of *King*
46 Cartoon studio that created Mr. Magoo, Gerald McBoing Boing
47 John Garfield did it—all the way
49 ". . . —— any drop to drink"
51 What Frances Farmer was to New York (1937 film)
55 Japanese sashes
57 Promissory note
59 American actor Moore in *Vivere in Pace* ("To Live in Peace"), *Paisan*
60 Walter ——, Phyllis Dietrichson's paramour
61 Belonging to Universal star of late thirties (*Dracula's Daughter, Tower of London, Sandy Is a Lady*)
64 He played Prime Minister Benjamin, Prince Faisal, King Charles I, Chancellor Adolf
65 Richard and Graham

(Solution on page 155)

DOWN

1 Mr. McCall, James Garner role
2 —— —— *Island With You*
3 His novels *Lust for Life, The President's Lady, The Agony and the Ecstasy* made into movies (init.)
4 B.R.'s Dr. Watson
5 Dine
6 Miss Adrian
7 River nymphs (Elizabethan spelling)
8 *Panic in the ——*, for short
9 Carol Reed thriller
10 Eagle's nest (var.)
11 Rex Harrison delineated the progress of one (*Notorious Gentleman* in U.S.)
12 Richard ——, actor specializing as Japanese "heavy" (*Wake Island, Tokyo Rose, First Yank Into Tokyo*)
18 Sphere
19 *Union ——*, for short
21 Rita played this gal
24 Letter in Old and Middle English
26 Joseph Wiseman played the evil Dr.
27 Cooper's was "good"; Lemmon's was a "good neighbor"
28 Southern state (abbr.)
29 Garfield starred in the play, Palance in the movie
30 George Montgomery Pacific adventure
32 Susan's title role in 1961 sudser
33 —— *Your Old Man*, with W.C. Fields
36 Forties leading lady (*Abie's Irish Rose, Red River*)
39 Actor with a gifted mule (init.)
40 She played Becky to Tommy's Tom
42 Billy Wilder's place for after-office hours high jinks, for short
43 Airport code for Brazil's largest city
45 —— *Hollywood*
47 Gossipy Miss Barrett
48 Character actor in *Arise, My Love* with catch phrase, "I'm not happy. I'm not happy at all."
50 Leo's sound
52 Film critic whose play *A Death in the Family* filmed as *All the Way Home*
53 "—— Who, —— You, —— I!", introduced by Will Osborne and his Orchestra in *Blues in the Night*
54 Financial offs.
56 Noncommissioned off.
58 French article
62 American cinematography pioneer, inventor of roll film (init.)
63 British star character actor (*Odd Man Out, Oliver Twist*) (init.)

TWO:
"...BUT WHO'S IN THE CAST?"

Sooner or later, in talking about any movie, most buffs will ask this question. A film may have a significant theme, skillful direction, and superb photography, but the lure of the performer remains most irresistible. There is an immutable magic in the movie camera that can transform a lucky actor or actress into a memorable screen presence: comic, sensual, tragic, or terrifying (and sometimes all four)—and we movie buffs will always respond with pleasure to that magic.

This section is about the movie players, old and new: their careers and their best roles. The first article concerns one of the grandest ladies the screen has ever given us: that redoubtable, irrepressible old darling, Margaret Rutherford.

ENGLAND'S
MOST FORMIDABLE DAME:
A Tribute to Margaret Rutherford

By Jerry Vermilye

BLITHE SPIRIT (1945). As Madame Arcati

In the annals of great movie character actresses, surely none is more cherished than Britain's Dame Margaret Rutherford. Famed for her lovably eccentric gallery of comedy characterizations, the actress presented a paradox not unusual in a profession celebrated for pigeonholing its successful performers and of making them re-create endless variations on past triumphs. For Dame Margaret's wistful, lifelong wish was to be a great dramatic actress in the grand tradition.

Her brilliance as a mistress of humor was clearly forecast by her resounding personal success in a 1935 stage comedy entitled *Short Story*, actor Robert Morley's debut as a playwright. The notices were uniform in their enchantment with Rutherford, and critic James Agate wrote: "There is no play to run off with, but if there were it would now be in the reticule of Miss Margaret Rutherford who, as a ruthless village spinster . . . entrances and

convulses the house every moment she is on the stage."

Yet, despite such successful variations into the dramatic repertoire as her Aline Solness in Donald Wolfit's 1934 revival of Ibsen's *The Master Builder*, and her sinister Mrs. Danvers (a role she created) in Daphne du Maurier's stage adaptation of her best-selling *Rebecca*, Rutherford remained a frustrated artist. As she once told an interviewer: "How I would love to have been a great traditional actress like Bernhardt, Duse or Ellen Terry. There have been so many parts I yearned to play." Indeed, the actress had to be literally coaxed into accepting some of the roles for which she is best remembered, including Madame Arcati in Noël Coward's *Blithe Spirit*, a part which she created on the stage in 1941 and repeated four years later for the screen. Nor was Miss Jane Marple, Agatha Christie's tweedy, irrepressible lady sleuth, a role which the actress initially found compatible. Ironically, it is quite possibly the characterization for which Margaret Rutherford is best remembered, internationally.

Dame Margaret was a late bloomer. Though obsessed with the idea of becoming an actress since an early success in childhood theatricals, she traveled many byways before making her 1933 West End stage debut at the somewhat advanced age of forty-one. The play was James Dale's melodramatic *Wild Justice*, and Rutherford's role was so insignificant that the critics passed her by. Before that, she had experienced years of amateur theatricals and repertory companies, and had even occasionally returned to her earlier profession of teaching piano.

Rutherford's appeal is universal and knows no age barrier. She is forceful, yet pliable—fierce, yet human. She has often been termed "bulldoglike" in appearance, and "tweedily eccentric" and "a splendidly padded windmill." In a 1967 television interview, Robert Morley offered a peer's informal tribute: "Although the profession is crowded with very nice people, she's almost too nice, too soft, too much the perfect auntie. She's frightfully funny. She's a marvelous woman . . . a good woman."

Outside of Britain, Dame Margaret is, of course, best known for her motion picture performances, although few today are familiar with her 1936 screen debut as Miss Butterby, the clever agent for a forgery gang in *Dusty Ermine*, in one scene of which the actress offered a forecast of films to come when she waylaid a detective with her lead-filled umbrella. For some time thereafter, she continued to accept character roles in equally forgettable films, while steadily honing her skills on the London stage.

On May 31, 1938, Margaret Rutherford's ambling career took a sharp upward turn when her performance in the charming comedy *Spring Meeting*, as a genteel Irish eccentric of seventy, bearing the singular name of "Bijou Furze," caused a sensation among both critics and public. Under John Gielgud's direction, she evolved a characterization that, while hilariously funny, at the same time bore a strong undercurrent of pathos. And Rutherford did not take easily to being laughed at.

Thus, at forty-six, she had become a full-fledged star and, in recognition of her new status, she was much photographed and written about in magazines and newspapers. Early in 1939, she was cast as Miss Prism in Gielgud's production of Oscar Wilde's *The Importance of Being Earnest*, with Gielgud himself as Jack Worthing and Edith Evans as Lady Bracknell. Again, Rutherford was much praised, and if there was, perhaps, a trace of Bijou Furze in her Prism, no one seemed to take exception. That September, with the world on the brink of war, London's theatres went temporarily dark.

The spring of 1940 saw the actress make a drastic switch from Wildean farce to melodrama as the grimly obsessed Mrs. Danvers, the evil housekeeper in Daphne du Maurier's stage adaptation of her romantic-Gothic best-seller, *Rebecca*. According to Eric Keown in his monograph on Rutherford's career: "Margaret Rutherford generated uncanny menace. It was an astonishing jump from Prism, and a triumph in that, although the author had pushed the character to the very brink of the ludicrous, so certain was the performance that it remained proof against even the involuntary titter."

After its West End engagement, *Rebecca* went on tour. One night in Exeter, Noël Coward visited backstage, bringing with him a copy of his newly completed comedy, *Blithe Spirit*. It contained, he announced, a marvelous role that he had tailored expressly for Rutherford—that of Madame Arcati, the bogus medium. The idea of making audiences laugh once again delighted her, and her only hesitation arose from her reluctance to risk offending professional mediums.

In July of 1941, *Blithe Spirit* opened in London, under Coward's direction, with a cast headed by Cecil Parker, Fay Compton and Kay Hammond. Having overcome her worries about satirizing spiritualists, Dame Margaret submerged herself in the part to the extent that she believed she was playing her straight. Having been coached by a famous medium prior to the production, she was overjoyed to discover, later on, that the profession actually appreciated her performance, chiefly for its very *avoidance* of burlesque.

Among the great hits of the London stage, *Blithe Spirit* ultimately tallied up a run of 1,997 performances. Ruther-

ford stayed with the cast little over a year. She never enjoyed long runs in plays, and once said, "About six months is right, I should think."

The first Margaret Rutherford film to promote international recognition of her work was her twelfth, David Lean's excellent screen version of *Blithe Spirit*. Wisely, Rutherford was retained from the original play, as was Kay Hammond's portrayal of the ectoplasmic Elvira, with Rex Harrison and Constance Cummings heading a flawless cast. One unforgettable embellishment on the original was the sight of Madame Arcati, her tweed cape billowing forth behind her, madly pedalling her bicycle over the Kentish countryside.

As the wildly absurd medium (Coward describes her as "a striking woman, dressed not too extravagantly but with a decided bias toward the barbaric"), Dame Margaret set a standard no other actress has yet been able to surpass or eradicate, despite numerous stage revivals, television productions, and even a musical version called *High Spirits*, with the illustrious Beatrice Lillie as Madame Arcati. The role remains irrevocably Rutherford's domain.

In the spring of 1945, the actress's admiration for actor-composer Ivor Novello and his brand of lavish musical fluff persuaded her to accept a small role in his *Perchance to Dream*. Early in the run, suddenly and impulsively, she and her old friend from repertory days, Stringer Davis, were married. The ceremony took place while Davis was home on leave from the service. Looking back on the event, Rutherford later remarked, "I was fifty-two. It was quite a romance."

In subsequent years, Davis and Rutherford were

THE HAPPIEST DAYS OF YOUR LIFE (1950). With Joyce Grenfell and Alastair Sim

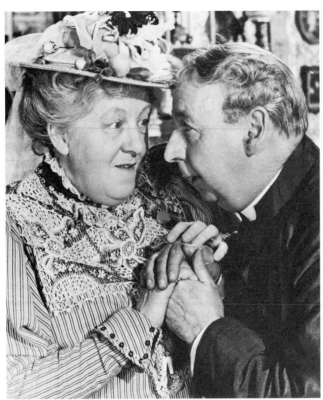

THE IMPORTANCE OF BEING EARNEST (1952). With Miles Malleson

seldom separated professionally, and he often accepted supporting or bit parts in her films, plays and theatre tours to Australia and the U.S. American audiences are likely most familiar with his continuing role as Miss Jane Marple's old-maidish foil and gentleman friend, "Mr. Stringer," in Rutherford's quartet of sixties mystery-comedies.

In 1947, Dame Margaret was on the screen as a French grande dame in *Meet Me at Dawn*, an inferior drama about duelling in *fin-de-siècle* Paris, and in the movie version of Terence Rattigan's play, *While the Sun Shines*, as a lady doctor. Then came the opportunity for her first trip to North America in a tour of *The Importance of Being Earnest*, with John Gielgud. This time, Rutherford was asked to leave Prism behind her for a second crack at Lady Bracknell, which she had first played years earlier at Oxford Playhouse.

But Dame Margaret was reluctant to play Bracknell now. She considered Edith Evans' portrayal the definitive interpretation, and she agreed to accept it only on the condition that she be allowed to wear exact copies of Evans' costumes and deliver a deliberate imitation of her predecessor's performance. In *The New York Times*, critic Brooks Atkinson wrote of her Lady Bracknell, "Miss Margaret Rutherford is tremendously skillful—the speaking, the walking and the wearing of costumes all gathered up into one impression of insufferability."

68

Five years later, in director Anthony Asquith's handsome 1952 color film of the Wilde classic, Evans and Rutherford once again offered their definitive versions of, respectively, Lady Bracknell and Miss Prism. Today, this interpretation of *Earnest* still glows as an ensemble job performed in great style by one and all, including perfect realizations of the two young couples by Michael Redgrave, Joan Greenwood, Dorothy Tutin and Michael Denison. It remains a jewel-box realization of an admittedly Victorian comedy-of-manners. But what impeccably *witty* manners!

Interesting insights into the Rutherford comedy style are offered by actor George Howe, who played featured roles with her in the fifties: "She did not know how funny she was being. She never strove to be funny and was always sincere in her approach to a comic part. She was an unconscious comic and just could not help being amusing. She had nervous tricks—she wrinkled her nose like a rabbit and she gobbled—and these mannerisms were encouraged by film directors, much to the delight of the public."

Dame Margaret's own seriousness of approach is borne out by a statement in her autobiography: "I have been told I was a natural clown and have been likened to Charlie Chaplin and Jacques Tati. I never think of myself that way. I play each role as I see it and always try to give it a new interpretation."

John Dighton's clever farce, *The Happiest Days of Your Life*, dealt hilariously with the fanciful postwar notion of a girls' school being billeted with a boys' school, through a miscalculation by the Ministry of Devacuation. With Rutherford as Miss Whitchurch, formidable headmistress of the girls' school, the comedy opened in London in March, 1948.

Two years later, she and Alastair Sim were happily teamed in that comedy's screen version, which certainly ranks among the memorable British comedies from that undefined "golden age" of English screen humor that vaguely ranges from 1945's *Blithe Spirit* to the early-sixties heyday of Peter Sellers. Not only was *Happiest Days*' mad lunacy carefully preserved, but Frank Launder's brilliant direction went further, expanding the action to fully utilize the possibilities of an entire school campus. Where the play had been confined to a single set, the movie ventured forth into the classrooms and playing fields, with uproariously inventive results, from interpretive Greek dancing on the lawns to roller-skating student-spies at large in the academic corridors. Margaret Rutherford was brilliant, striding bullishly through the ivied halls in her sensible, tweedy suits and capes and mortarboard hat, parrying stratagems with Sim in a bluff, soldierly manner that contrasted perfectly with his familiar crushed charm. Their endless duel of wits and words is nicely set off against the gurgling enthusiasm of Joyce Grenfell's athletics instructor.

From the film's credits, appropriately embellished by

the priceless drawings of Ronald ("The Belles of St. Trinian's") Searle, to the intricate plan-of-action devised to prevent visiting girls' parents from spotting the boy students (and vice versa), the film is the epitome of great British farce, featuring innocent double-entendres (Headmistress Rutherford to headmaster Sim, upon her arrival: "How many mistresses have you?") and clever sight gags (school custodian Edward Rigby, faced with the logistics of constantly switching playing-field equipment from rugby to lacrosse, and back again—and again). And always, attempting to deal with this inventive comedy-of-a-million-errors are the lugubrious Sim and the determined, imperious Rutherford, harassed but never quite defeated by the chaos that surrounds them. *The Happiest Days of Your Life* is a priceless bit of vintage nonsense, and it's a pity that the film is now so rarely shown. It's interesting to note that during the 1957-58 season, Rutherford and Stringer Davis toured Australia with the play. The role was obviously, and understandably, among her favorites.

By the early fifties, Margaret Rutherford in a film's cast was, for American art-house audiences, the female equivalent of an Alec Guinness. Their names ensured a pleasurable and skilled display of comic craft, whether or not the attendant vehicle was worthy of them. Unlike Guinness, however, the Rutherford characterizations were seldom of central significance to the plot. Instead they served to augment and enrich a screenplay, and provide that memorably eccentric imprint of fine character work so indelibly patented by the British.

Thus, one recalls with delight Dame Margaret's inimitably whacky, matter-of-fact Nurse Carey in *Miranda* (and its sequel, *Mad About Men*), engaged to attend to the needs of dry-landed mermaid Glynis Johns; her unusual history professor in *Passport to Pimlico*, in which the discovery of a 15th-century charter proves London's Pimlico district to be an actual part of Burgundy; as a spinster painter, delightfully paired with Stringer Davis, in *Innocents in Paris*; the strongminded amateur playwright who clashes head-on with rep-company director Robert Morley in *Curtain Up*; the genteel, delightful lady shoplifter, blithely "picking up a few bargains" in *Trouble in Store*; as *Miss Robin Hood*, a nutty collector of children and birds who purloins a secret whiskey formula; and as the ancient box-office "girl" of *The Smallest Show on Earth*, a thoroughly charming little tale about a young couple who inherit a run-down cinema in a Northern Britain industrial town. These, and at least a dozen other Rutherford creations, remain in the memory, often long after the movies themselves have been forgotten.

Agatha Christie admitted to having had Margaret Rutherford in mind when she created the character of Miss Jane Marple, amateur detective, in a series of mystery novels and stories. Vain efforts had previously been made to engage the actress to portray this character in a play or film, but she had always resisted. Indeed,

Dame Margaret staunchly balked at the thought of taking part in any murder mystery, declaring, "Murder, you see, is not the sort of thing I can get close to. I don't like these things that are just for thrills. I would far rather go without work. I do not like murder. It has an atmosphere I have always found uncongenial."

But a shortage of suitable roles and a friend's gentle persuasion that a thriller need not only entertain, but could also have a moral value, eventually caused her to accept MGM's offer of the starring role in a series of Miss Marple adventures, adapted from the Christie fictions. The first of these movies, initially entitled *Meet Miss Marple*, but released as *Murder She Said*, derived from the novel *4:50 From Paddington*. It evolved from a train journey during which the energetic, elderly sleuth sees a woman murdered on a passing train, then sets out to investigate and track down the murderer by becoming a servant at a country estate. In this, as in each of the subsequent Marple pictures, Stringer Davis played "Mr. Stringer," the village librarian and more of an old maid than Miss Marple herself, yet a perfect foil for Rutherford in her sleuthing.

On film, the originally birdlike, literary Miss Jane Marple was somewhat altered and toughened up to suit Margaret Rutherford's vigorous style of dry good

MURDER AT THE GALLOP (1963). With Robert Morley

69

THE V.I.P.s (1963). With Orson Welles

humor. All the ingredients appeared to work; to the tune of Ron Goodwin's jaunty background score, *Murder She Said* scored a tremendous success, not only in Britain and the U.S., but all over the world.

The Marple series came at a time when Rutherford had severely felt the bite of income taxes. She explained to an interviewer, "As I was finishing my last play, I suddenly realized that I shouldn't have any income in the near future and the government was taking every penny I earned. I called my accountant person in and said to him, 'Don't pay another penny until I tell you to. I can't afford this sort of thing!'" Further protesting the high taxation of performers, she remarked, "If they raise the taxes once again, I shall go to jail. I don't want to leave this country, my home, as others I know have done, because they have taxed me beyond endurance. I would make a stand before I would let myself be driven out by the outrageous impositions of the tax authorities. Some of us have to mark the line somewhere."

In 1963, having become wiser to the ways in which some show people solve their tax problems, she officially became Margaret Rutherford, Ltd.. This was a banner year for the Rutherford screen career; she signed a term-contract with MGM, and had important roles in three films. In *The Mouse on the Moon*, a slapdash little sequel to Peter Sellers' *The Mouse That Roared*, she replaced him as Gloriana, Grand Duchess of Grand Fenwick. But

her role was smallish and, suffering from an uninspired script, this *Mouse* seemed mild and labored.

Murder at the Gallop, though derived from Agatha Christie's Hercule Poirot novel *After the Funeral*, nevertheless adapted well to the requirements of the Marple series. And Margaret Rutherford, capably supported by Robert Morley and Flora Robson, was once again a delight as the elderly but persistent bloodhound with the billowing cape, tracking a murderer in and about a fashionable hotel/riding school called The Gallop. In one scene, partnered by the equally formidable Morley, she even danced an amusing Twist.

Murder at the Gallop remains the most interesting and entertaining of the four Marple films, which sadly declined with the two subsequent mysteries, *Murder Most Foul* and *Murder Ahoy*. Two years later, she made a fleeting gag appearance as Miss Marple—and the one bright spot—in another Agatha Christie movie, the otherwise forgettable *The Alphabet Murders*.

Dame Margaret won her only Oscar, as Best Supporting Actress of 1963, for her Duchess of Brighton in Anthony Asquith's *The V.I.P.s*. A latter-day *Grand Hotel*, Terence Rattigan's star-laden plot concerns a group of airline passengers whose flight to the U.S. is held up by a London fog, and of the critical effect this delay has on certain passengers' lives. Rutherford's Duchess is en route to Florida to serve as a resort hostess, apparently her only hope of earning the money to maintain her impoverished family estate. Constantly popping an array of tranquilizers and stay-awake pills, she remarks to an attendant (the ubiquitous Stringer Davis), "I shall clearly arrive in Florida in an advanced state of drug addiction!"

This performance contains all the wonderful technical trickery the public had come to expect of Dame Margaret; watch how she delivers a line, pauses, and forms a small "O" with her mouth as she freezes that formidable jaw, often with a sidelong glance or upraised eyebrow. And she even carries off the ridiculous without making it seem corny (i.e., seated on the plane, she responds to the loudspeaker's "Kindly fasten your seatbelts" with an honestly agitated "But I haven't *brought* a seat belt!").

A poignant figure, the Duchess is eventually saved from her much-feared debut flight by the plot contrivance of having a fellow passenger (Orson Welles' film magnate) elect to use her ancestral estate as the location for his next movie—for a handsome rental fee.

In 1961, Rutherford had been honored by Queen Elizabeth by receiving the Order of the British Empire (O.B.E.), and with the Queen's New Year's honors list of 1967, she was officially awarded the title of "Dame" Margaret Rutherford. By then, coincidentally, her career was near its unfortunate end. In her final decade, Dame Margaret suffered numerous nervous breakdowns. "My nerves aren't the best," she once told a reporter. "Work can be a cure, but psychiatry saved me. Analysis is a godsend." She claimed that a doctor-friend once told her she could thank her nerves for the accomplishments of her career.

In a 1964 *Time* magazine interview, Rutherford referred to a recent breakdown: "I went quite scatty. Fortunately, I was playing a scatty part in a play, so nobody noticed."

But her fellow-workers *did* take notice. In 1965, she appeared in a West End production of *The Solid Gold Cadillac*, commuting back and forth from a nursing home to the theatre, where a doctor remained always in attendance backstage. Making her initial stage entrance at each performance apparently required great courage of the 73-year-old actress, and the play's run became as upsetting for the other cast members as it did for Dame Margaret herself. In addition, she was plagued with the fear that she would forget her lines and that the stage manager might have to ring down the curtain in the middle of a scene.

Among her last film roles, she portrayed an impressive Mistress Quickly (a brief part) in Orson Welles' *Chimes at Midnight (Falstaff)*, in which she gives a superb recounting of the death of Falstaff. She is also briefly effective as an irritably seasick passenger in Charles Chaplin's pathetically unfunny *A Countess From Hong Kong*. But in the Italian-made comedy *Arabella*, a stylish but empty Virna Lisi vehicle, one sees sad evidence of Rutherford's all-too obvious decline. Again, she portrays a wealthy dowager whose fortunes have dwindled, but her lines are delivered so deliberately, with such solemnity, and with none of the old Rutherford ginger, that one can almost see the cue cards being held up off-camera to enable Dame Margaret to recall her dialogue. While filming in Italy in 1966, Rutherford broke her hip in an accident from which, reportedly, she never fully recovered.

Earlier that year, while playing Mrs. Malaprop in a London revival of *The Rivals*, she had shown signs of failing memory, and admitted that she occasionally had to make up some of her own Malapropisms, since she could not always remember Sheridan's exact lines.

In 1969, Dame Margaret was contracted for cameo roles in two movies she was never to film: *Song of Norway* and *The Virgin and the Gypsy*. In the latter, she was to have played the deaf old grandmother who, despite her ever-present ear-trumpet, disrupts dinner-table conversation by misconstruing words and requiring reiterated sentences. The role was relatively brief but quite amusing, and one that Rutherford would ordinarily have been able to sail through with little effort, but profound comic effect. But no longer. Unfortunately, the film was being shot on a very tight schedule, with studio facilities available for only a few days' time. And, because she suffered constant lapses of memory, Dame Margaret's scenes had to be shot and re-shot, over and over. Finally, it was decided that another actress must be engaged, and Fay Compton was hired to replace her. Sadly, that marked the end of Rutherford's career.

In the last years before her death on May 23, 1972, aged 80, Dame Margaret had retreated into another world altogether, with Stringer Davis ever present to attend to her needs. Fifteen months thereafter, desolate without his wife, he too passed away.

Although, like most fine actors, Margaret Rutherford preferred the stage to the screen, it is fortunate that so much of her best work is preserved on film. Thus, her great comic gifts remain available both for audience appreciation and as an invaluable guide for students of the art of playing comedy. An expert technician, Rutherford spent half her lifetime learning and perfecting the timing and the character traits required for her inimitable gallery of eccentric ladies. A born romantic, the actress adored poetry and often gave readings for church and civic organizations. And, despite the fact that she regretted and resented the physical characteristics that prevented her from being a true first lady of the theatre—that made her, instead, a clown—she learned to cope with her lot and capitalize on her handicaps, such as they were.

In private life, Dame Margaret's appearance was often as unconventional as her on-screen persona, and she favored billowing cloaks, colorful dress patterns and loud costume jewelry. Friends claim that this was no affectation; Rutherford was merely being herself, and could, therefore, get away with it without seeming in the least ridiculous. Assuredly, there has never been another performer quite like Margaret Rutherford, and it seems doubtful that we shall ever see her formidable, fierce-jawed, magnificently eccentric like again.

MURDER AHOY (1964). With husband Stringer Davis

THE NAME GAME (TWO)

In the first *Movie Buff's Book*, this quiz proved to be so popular that we thought it deserved an encore. Below is a list of well-known actors and actresses, using their *true* names and citing their less familiar movies. How many of these players can you identify?

1. Suzanne Burce in *Athena* (1954)
2. Bernard Zanville in *That Way With Women* (1947)
3. Zelma Hedrick in *Rio Rita* (1942)
4. Sophia Kosow in *Merrily We Go to Hell* (1932)
5. Benjamin Kubelsky in *Artists and Models* (1937)
6. Ella Geisman in *Her Highness and the Bellboy* (1945)
7. John Hamilton in *Battle Taxi* (1955)
8. Arthur Gelien in *Island of Desire* (1952)
9. William Joseph Shields in *Tarzan's Secret Treasure* (1941)
10. Peggy Middleton in *River Lady* (1948)
11. Betty Joan Perske in *Bright Leaf* (1950)
12. Jake Krantz in *Mandalay* (1934)
13. Ira Grossel in *Flame of Araby* (1951)
14. Pauline Levy in *The Lady Has Plans* (1942)
15. Jane Peters in *No More Orchids* (1934)
16. Elizabeth Thornburg in *Spring Reunion* (1957)
17. Leila Von Koerber in *Reducing* (1931)
18. Leonard Slye in *The Cowboy and the Senorita* (1944)
19. Harlean Carpenter in *Personal Property* (1937)
20. Natasha Gurdin in *Chicken Every Sunday* (1948)
21. Alexandra Zuck in *The Wild and the Innocent* (1959)
22. Ann LaHiff in *Child of Manhattan* (1933)
23. Margaret Reed in *College Swing* (1938)
24. Lucille Le Sueur in *Letty Lynton* (1932)
25. Rosita Alverio in *Latin Lovers* (1953)

(Answers on page 155)

Bernard Schwartz and Rosetta Jacobs* in SON OF ALI BABA (1952).

*also known as Tony Curtis and Piper Laurie

FROM THE PAGES OF HISTORY

Each item below lists three historical or actual persons, all of whom were played by *one* actor or actress. You are asked to name that actor or actress, and the film in which he/she played each of the roles.

1. a) Sigmund Romberg b) Alfred Dreyfus c) Toulouse-Lautrec

2. a) King Louis XVI b) W.S. Gilbert c) King George III

3. a) Texas Guinan b) Pearl White c) Blossom Seeley

4. a) Andrew Jackson b) John the Baptist c) Gen. Charles Gordon

5. a) Robert Browning b) Mark Twain c) Christopher Columbus

6. a) Ferdinand W. Demara, Jr. b) Ira Hayes c) Albert DeSalvo

7. a) Jim Corbett b) John Barrymore c) George Custer

8. a) Thomas Edison b) Lorenz Hart c) "Baby Face" Nelson

9. a) Jane Froman b) Rachel Jackson c) Lillian Roth

10. a) Edwin Booth b) Thomas à Becket c) King Henry VIII

11. a) Billie Burke b) Katie O'Shea c) Ann Gilbreth

12. a) Clarence Darrow b) Benjamin Franklin c) Cardinal Wolsey

13. a) Napoleon III b) Napoleon Bonaparte c) David Belasco

14. a) Pierre Curie b) J. J. Shubert c) Florenz Ziegfeld

15. a) George S. Kaufman b) Al Capone c) Doc Holliday

16. a) Benjamin Disraeli b) King Charles I c) Adolf Hitler

17. a) Gustave Flaubert b) General Edwin Rommel c) Emperor Franz-Josef

18. a) Lon Chaney b) Admiral William Halsey c) Martin "the Gimp" Snyder

19. a) King Henry VIII b) Rembrandt van Rijn c) King Henry VIII (again)

20. Here is a final bicentennial question: Match the historical figure of America's Old West with the actor who played him. (Can you also name the film in which he played the role?)

a) Davy Crockett	a) Chuck Connors
b) Sam Houston	b) Robert Taylor
c) Jim Bowie	c) Joel McCrea
d) "Buffalo Bill" Cody	d) John Wayne
e) Jesse James	e) Gary Cooper
f) Geronimo	f) Alan Ladd
g) Wyatt Earp	g) J. Carrol Naish
h) Sitting Bull	h) Richard Dix
i) Billy the Kid	i) Robert Wagner
j) Wild Bill Hickok	j) James Stewart

(Answers on page 156)

Bonus Photo Question:
American ambassador Joseph E. Davies (Walter Huston) meets England's Prime Minister Winston Churchill (Dudley Field Malone) in a scene from which controversial wartime movie?

HALF-WAY UP THE LADDER

In this quiz, you are asked to identify a group of actresses who were talented and attractive women but who never really made it to full-fledged stardom. (If you can name at least ten, you are graced with a first-class movie memory.)

Photo 1
She made her debut in 1940 as the heroine to Cesar Romero's Cisco Kid in THE GAY CABALLERO, then went on to make minor movies, mostly for Fox, throughout the forties. (She appeared twice with Laurel and Hardy.) Here she is in LADIES OF WASHINGTON, with Anthony Quinn.

Photo 2
This capable actress had a number of important roles in such films as SCARFACE (1932), DINNER AT EIGHT (1933), and OUR DAILY BREAD (1934). In this photograph from THE GIRL FROM SCOTLAND YARD (1937), she is engaged in serious discussion with Eduardo Ciannelli.

Photo 3
A leading or supporting player in minor films, this actress made her debut in the movie pictured here: LADY OF BURLESQUE (1943), with Barbara Stanwyck and Charles Dingle.

Photo 4
A pert brunette, this lady appeared in a number of late-thirties programmers. She never achieved stardom at Warners, but she was James Cagney's leading lady in CEILING ZERO (1935).

Photo 5
This British-born actress was the heroine of many forties features, often pursued by unearthly creatures out for no good. (THE WOLF MAN was her best-known nemesis.) Here she appears with Turhan Bey (TURHAN BEY?) in THE MAD GHOUL (1943).

Photo 6
A leading lady in mostly minor movies of the forties, this attractive actress could be prominently seen in DESTROYER (1943), PARDON MY PAST (1945), and (above) COUNTER-ATTACK, with Paul Muni.

Photo 7
This pretty actress only appeared in films from 1949 to 1951 but she made an impression with her warmth and sincerity. She was at her best as Arthur Kennedy's sympathetic girlfriend in BRIGHT VICTORY (1951). Here she is in a 1950 movie, WOMAN IN HIDING, with Ida Lupino.

Photo 8
A charming heroine of the late thirties, this actress was featured in SOULS AT SEA (1937), LAST TRAIN FROM MADRID (1937), and SAY IT IN FRENCH (1938). In this photograph, she appears (at the right) with Frances Farmer, an unusually talented actress of the period, in SOUTH OF PAGO PAGO (1940).

Photo 9
Usually appearing in low-budget musicals, this actress made her debut with Abbott and Costello in BUCK PRIVATES (1941). (It was also their first film.) Here she is seen with Richard Arlen and "Gabby" Hayes in a scene from THE BIG BONANZA (1945).

Photo 10
With her throaty voice and rather lugubrious manner, this actress was ideal for troubled heroines. (She was one of the FOUR DAUGHTERS featured in the popular Warners' series.) In this scene, she appears with Milburn Stone and Humphrey Bogart in CRIME SCHOOL (1938). A few years later, she was his anguished wife in THEY DRIVE BY NIGHT (1940).

Photo 11
The actress was prominently featured at Warners in the forties, notably in HOTEL BERLIN (1945) and THE MAN I LOVE (1946). This photograph shows her in a scene from Warner's partly risible, partly frightening melodrama, THE BEAST WITH FIVE FINGERS in 1946.

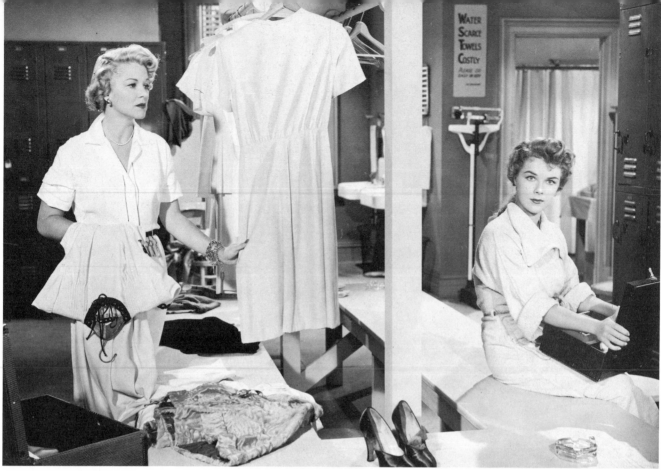

Photo 12
A leading lady of the early fifties, the actress at the right appeared in MYSTERY STREET (1950), EXCUSE MY DUST (1951), among other films. Here, in HARD, FAST, AND BEAUTIFUL (1951), she is a tennis player being victimized by ambitious mother Claire Trevor.

Photo 13
This actress starred in many forties movies, including PHANTOM LADY (1943), HAIL THE CONQUERING HERO (1944), and THE SUSPECT (1945). In this scene from BRUTE FORCE (1947), she appears with Whit Bissell.

Photo 14
The vivacious actress shown here with Glenn Ford and Claire Trevor in THE ADVENTURES OF MARTIN EDEN (1942) made many movies, but she is probably best remembered as Julie Benson (surrogate for Ruby Keeler) in THE JOLSON STORY (1946).

Photo 15
A scene from Josef von Sternberg's bizarre 1941 drama, THE SHANGHAI GESTURE, with Victor Mature, Gene Tierney, and an actress who appeared in over two dozen movies in the thirties and forties. This was probably her best role. Her name?

Photo 16
This vivacious actress made a number of movies in the late thirties and early forties, mostly at Fox (SECOND HONEYMOON, 1937; SALLY, IRENE AND MARY, 1938; THREE BLIND MICE, 1938, etc.). In this scene from LEAVE IT TO BLONDIE (1945), she appears with Chick Chandler and Arthur ("Dagwood") Lake.

Photo 17
Throughout the forties and into the fifties, this exceptionally attractive actress (center) was featured in many movies, often as wicked or "other" women. Here is a scene from THE POWER OF THE WHISTLER (1945), in which she is flanked by Tala Birell and Richard Dix.

(Answers on page 156)

Photo 18
A highly appealing and pretty heroine in scores of films, this actress made her debut in 1932 and retired in the mid-forties. Among her best-known movies: THE INVISIBLE MAN (1933), GOLD DIGGERS OF 1935 (1935), and THE PRISONER OF SHARK ISLAND (1936). This scene with Reginald Owen is from a very minor opus, THE GIRL ON THE FRONT PAGE (1936).

YOU STILL HAVE RELATIVES IN CHERMANY?:
The Suave Villains of World War II

by Lee Edward Stern

The screen Nazis of the World War II movies were a fascinating lot, many of them more interesting and complex than the stars who played the heroes. Unlike the Japanese villains, who were pictured as sneaky, buck-toothed, fanatically dedicated monsters whose greatest joy was to rape and kill, the Germans were frequently depicted as smooth, cultivated opportunists or jaded philosophers who loved good wine, good food, and good music. Nevertheless, they didn't turn a hair when they were "forced" to threaten retaliation against relatives or friends in Germany, or to massacre innocent villagers at random to prevent an open rebellion. (One of the rare exceptions to the usual Hollywood portrayal of the Japanese monster was Richard Loo's oily commander in *The Purple Heart* [1944], who hissed his way convincingly through such classic lines as "I wass educated in your U.C.L.A.," managing to make the L sound like a barely altered R).

But the Nazis truly triggered the writers' and actors' imaginations, resulting in a colorful and compelling roster of villains we loved to hate. Some of the casting was obvious: suave, sinister Conrad Veidt; powerful, masterly Erich von Stroheim; Otto Preminger, sneering

and arrogant long before he became a noted director; lithe, lizard-like Martin Kosleck, who made a small career out of playing Joseph Goebbels and lesser Nazi luminaries; the incomparable, unforgettable Peter Lorre. Veidt, von Stroheim, and Preminger, in particular, wore their ever-present monocles with the calm assurance of Prussian drillmasters. But other, more offbeat casting led to some wonderful moments—the usually lovable little Ludwig Stossel happily pushing Walter Pidgeon over a cliff in *Man Hunt* (1941), that wonderful suspense-thriller about the big-game hunter who sets out to prove he can assassinate Hitler: twinkly-eyed Edmund Gwenn failing in his attempt to shove Joel McCrea off a cathedral tower in Alfred Hitchcock's *Foreign Correspondent* (1940). (He topples over himself.)

Although many of the screen villains had authentic German or Continental accents, many others were recognizably English or American. Sir Cedric Hardwicke, George Sanders, Herbert Marshall, Raymond Massey, Basil Rathbone and others wore *their* monocles as naturally and proudly as their European colleagues. And Sydney Greenstreet brought his bulk and chortle to the service of the Fuehrer in several picturesque portrayals, notably in *Passage to Marseille* (1944). All of these actors played both sides of the game, sometimes appearing as high-ranking Allied officials or patriots, sometimes as German spies or officers.

Among the many other smoothies who taunted the Allied forces, and whose methodical brilliance was no match for the more erratic, irrepressible, unpredictable American or British heroes, were Henry Daniell, George Zucco, Otto Kruger, and Carl Esmond. Shuttling frequently from A to B movies and back again, they pitted themselves against such familiar fictional protagonists as Sherlock Holmes (oddly transported in time), Tarzan, Maisie (remember Ann Sothern as the wise-cracking blonde?), and Charlie Chan.

Of the villains with American accents (or carefully cultivated theatrical ones), John Carradine was one of the most ubiquitous. In *Man Hunt*, which was chock full of fascinating characters and action sequences, Carradine stood out as the killer with the sword-umbrella. Unfortunately, his talents were frequently wasted on such bombs as *Hitler's Madman* (1943), in which he hammily played the infamous Nazi exterminator, Reinhard Heydrich. The virtually unknown Hans von Twardowski,

MAN HUNT (1941). With George Sanders as Major Quive-Smith, preparing to stalk Walter Pidgeon

a real-life refugee from Hitler's Germany, was much more effective in the same role in Fritz Lang's *Hangmen Also Die*, released the same year.

As far back as 1939, *Confessions of a Nazi Spy* was widely heralded as a pioneering Hollywood anti-Nazi film. Although based on fact, it was considered daring because of its implications that murderous Fascists were operating from consulates in the U.S.. At any rate, Edward G. Robinson's strong, solid FBI man was more than a match for the evil machinations of a striking Nazi group headed by George Sanders, Paul Lukas, and a frightened, reluctant Francis Lederer.

Many of the most famous anti-war films were turned out before the United States officially entered the war in 1941. *Foreign Correspondent*, *Escape*, *The Mortal Storm*, and Charlie Chaplin's *The Great Dictator* were all released in 1940, and *Man Hunt* was written and produced before the Japanese attack on Pearl Harbor. Of all these, only *Foreign Correspondent* and *Man Hunt* have stood the test of time. In *Escape*, the acting honors were shared by Conrad Veidt and the former silent screen star, Alla Nazimova, who made her sound debut as the German actress imprisoned in a concentration camp but rescued by her American son, Robert Taylor. The film barely escapes from complete boredom only because of the strong acting by Veidt, who easily overpowers Taylor in their scenes together.

In MGM's *The Mortal Storm*, three unlikely young Germans (Robert Young, James Stewart, and Robert Stack) are caught up in the maelstrom of Nazism and forced to examine their own philosophies. Frank Morgan stands out as a "non-Aryan," anti-Hitler professor who is sent to a concentration camp, while his stepsons, Robert Stack and Robert Young, are converted to the Hitlerian theories. Only daughter Margaret Sullavan and her fiancé James Stewart defy the Nazis and are shot down as they try to flee Germany.

The semi-comic villains in Chaplin's celebrated misfire, *The Great Dictator*, were, of course, played by such famous comedians as Jack Oakie and Chaplin himself. The film's heart was in the right place, but script and direction were broad, crude, and essentially simple-minded. Ironically, the familiar and always dependable Henry Daniell, who played it straight, was much more compelling than either Chaplin or Oakie.

A much more successful anti-Nazi comedy was Ernst Lubitsch's *To Be Or Not To Be* (1942), in which Jack Benny was at his best as a touring Shakespearian actor caught with his troupe of players in occupied Poland. Benny traded honors and laughs not only with Carole Lombard, in what was to be her last screen appearance, but with the hilarious Sig Rumann, again playing one of his choleric Nazis. His bluster and eloquent eyebrows were never again utilized quite so successfully.

Probably the most famous and most-talked-about cult movie of the war years, *Casablanca*, also made its

NAZI AGENT (1942). With Martin Kosleck and Conrad Veidt

BERLIN CORRESPONDENT (1942). With Martin Kosleck and Mona Maris

85

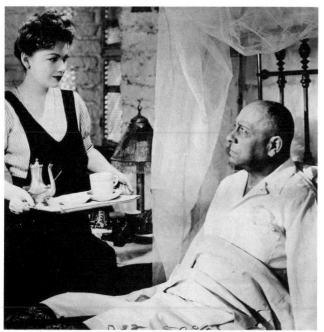

FIVE GRAVES TO CAIRO (1943). With Anne Baxter and
Erich von Stroheim

appearance in 1942. It featured a complete gallery of
villains and ambiguous opportunists, all of them wonder-
fully portrayed: Conrad Veidt's indomitable Nazi major;
Peter Lorre's wretched little turncoat, with his acidulous
exchange with Humphrey Bogart—"You despise me,
Rick, don't you?" "If I gave you any thought I probably
would"; Claude Rains' charming, but corrupt and oppor-
tunistic, police officer; Sydney Greenstreet's familiar fat
villain, complete with fez and fan, swindling his way
through the war.

Veidt and Lorre appeared also that year in *All Through
the Night*, in which they were joined in their Nazi
skulduggery by a cold and venomous Judith Anderson.
Her steely glance was enough to convince us all that she
would do anything—*anything*—for the Fatherland. (The
following year, in *Edge of Darkness*, she changed sides,
playing a Norwegian patriot who unhappily falls in love
with a German soldier.)

Hitchcock's second-rate *Saboteur* has Norman Lloyd
as a slippery Nazi agent who is pursued by desperate hero
Robert Cummings all over the country. Cummings, falsely accused of the crime of sabotage committed by Lloyd,
finally tracks his prey to the Statue of Liberty. Fleeing
from Cummings, Lloyd falls and hangs precariously from
an edge of the statue. As Cummings clutches the dangling
Lloyd with one hand, the agent's jacket rips at the seam,
sending him toppling to his death. (Lloyd later gave up
villainy to become a producer, mainly for Hitchcock.)

Meanwhile, in *Mrs. Miniver*, Greer Garson's stiff-
upper-lip British housewife had very little trouble cap-

turing a confused, downed German pilot, played by dour
but handsome Helmut Dantine. Dantine followed this
debut with a series of interesting Nazi villains, particularly in *Edge of Darkness* and *Northern Pursuit* (both 1943).
In *Escape in the Desert* (1945), an updated remake of *The
Petrified Forest*, he played an escaped Nazi war criminal
who traps a group of people in an isolated diner.

Conrad Veidt displayed his virtuosity in a dual role in
1942's *Nazi Agent*, in which he appeared as a pair of
twins—one a German-born American patriot, the other a
Nazi bigwig. The helpful Martin Kosleck added a touch
of menace as an underling, and the smooth direction was
by Jules Dassin.

In 1943, Basil Rathbone's razor-sharp features (he was
once accurately described as looking like two profiles
pasted together) and clipped accent were two of the major
attractions of *Above Suspicion*, with good guys Fred
MacMurray and Joan Crawford on a mission to Germany—to find a secret formula. MacMurray was sup-
posed to be, believe it or not, an Oxford don on holiday.
Rathbone, MacMurray's former colleague but now in the
Gestapo, was a truly cultivated villain, complete with an
addiction to classical music and quiet torture.

That same year saw Sir Cedric Hardwicke in an effec-
tively underplayed performance as a cultivated, intellec-
tually torn German commander in John Steinbeck's story
of the heroic resistance of Norwegian villagers, *The Moon
Is Down*.

With the war at its height, 1943 brought a bumper crop
of anti-Nazi films. Martin Kosleck and Erich von
Stroheim were at their sadistic best in Lewis Milestone's
North Star, in which von Stroheim wore his fabled mono-
cle and removed his ever-present gloves with stunning
grace, while Kosleck almost licked his chops as a physi-
cian who takes blood from Russian children for
transfusions to wounded German soldiers.

One of the stalwart members of the Russian family
menaced by von Stroheim and company in *North Star*
was Anne Baxter, who appeared opposite von Stroheim
(as a gangster-like Rommel) later that year in the flawed
but fascinating *Five Graves to Cairo*. In this highly fic-
tionalized account of the Desert Fox's comeuppance,
Miss Baxter joined Franchot Tone, a British officer posing as a Nazi, in outwitting the formidable general while
he was quartered in a flea-bag African hotel.

The movie version of Lillian Hellman's famous stage
play, *Watch on the Rhine*, was dominated by a quartet of
male actors with a quartet of accents. Although Bette
Davis, the biggest Warner Brothers' star of the period,
was disappointingly colorless as the wife of the hero, Paul
Lukas played her German anti-Fascist husband with
Academy-award-winning flair. His brilliant performance
was matched by that of the versatile Anglo-American
George Coulouris, as a vicious informer; and by two of
the meanest villains of them all, bald-headed, eye-rolling
Kurt Katch and velvet-voiced Henry Daniell.

While Lukas was eluding his Nazi pursuers, the sleek and implacable Walter Slezak was hounding Charles Laughton, the quietly brave schoolmaster in Jean Renoir's *This Land Is Mine*, a well-intentioned but labored picture about the German occupation of an unnamed country resembling France.

A year later, Slezak was back as the clever Nazi who outthought and outplanned all the other survivors of the sinking of a ship in Alfred Hitchcock's *Lifeboat*. Sometimes, those of us in the audience wondered if our side could really be winning the war, since our adversaries seemed far more clever than the would-be good guys. Who could help but admire Slezak when he alone was smart enough to secrete a cache of vitamins and water in the crowded lifeboat? His gloating was annoying, but his adroitness was admirable. It seemed unfair of his boatmates to throw him into the ocean as a reward for his foresight.

(Not that the heroes were all blundering idiots. Remember the cool ingenuity of *Man Hunt*'s Walter Pidgeon, trapped in a cave by the sly, smooth-talking George Sanders, silently fashioning a makeshift bow and arrow from a belt and a pen while distracting his tormentor with a philosophical conversation?)

In 1944, all the famous Nazi war criminals were brought together fictionally for John Farrow's *The Hitler Gang*, a well-reasoned but unexciting examination of how the Nazis took over Germany. Martin Kosleck was his usual effective self as Goebbels, but Robert Watson, a Hitler look-alike, was woefully weak in what should have been the pivotal role. (Watson played Hitler throughout the war years, usually in such execrable nonsense as *The Devil With Hitler* and *That Nazty Nuisance*.)

In 1945, Vicki Baum reworked her familiar Grand Hotel formula for *Hotel Berlin*, in which the egotistical Raymond Massey, as a German officer desperately trying to escape from Hitler's collapsing regime, was confounded by Helmut Dantine, as a disguised underground leader. Who could blame Massey for being foiled, after Dantine had played so many Nazis in other films of the period? Peter Lorre also switches sides in this one, and steals the film as a somewhat hysterical anti-Nazi professor trying to vainly find "the good German" he has heard so much about.

The end of World War II did not automatically bring an end to the reign of anti-Nazi films. Two of the best, *The House on 92nd Street* (1945) and *The Stranger* (1946) were released after the war. Among the Nazi spies in that famous house—the meeting place for subversives—were Leo G. Carroll, Gene Lockhart, and the beautiful Signe Hasso, who so often in the past had fought and suffered for the Allies.

In *The Stranger*, Orson Welles directed and starred in a suspenseful vehicle designed to demonstrate that, although the fighting on the battlefields was over, the fight for the control of minds was continuing. The powerful portrayal by Welles, of a war criminal hiding out from the Allied War Crimes Commission by posing as a teacher in a small New England town, was paralleled by that of Edward G. Robinson, as the G-man who penetrates his disguise and causes his downfall. In a well-remembered and highly theatrical finale, Welles is trapped in the tower holding the town's huge clock and meets his doom by being impaled on the sword held by a revolving metal knight.

The dozens of films featuring the screen villains of World War II were very popular in their day, but that day—when it was oh, so easy to spot heroes and villains, to know which to cheer and which to boo and hiss—is past. Very few of these movies deserve the status of classics—with the obvious exceptions of *Casablanca*, perhaps *Foreign Correspondent* and *Man Hunt*, and possibly *To Be Or Not To Be*. But the memorable gallery of screen portraits brought to life by the great character actors of that day will continue to tantalize and delight us as long as we have memories and television sets.

LIFEBOAT (1944). With John Hodiak, Walter Slezak, Tallulah Bankhead, and Hume Cronyn

"THIS KID HAS TALENT!"

This quiz is a personal tribute to the stars of movie musicals who, as the expression goes, "sang and danced their way into our hearts." A few of them may have lost some of their original lustre, but for the pleasure they brought us, for the sheer exhilaration of their best moments on film, they will be remembered.

Alice Faye: Limited in acting ability and not exactly sparkling as a personality, she nevertheless had a blonde prettiness, a throaty voice, and a charming pout that made her an endearing musical heroine.

1. In which movie did she give a fetching rendition of "This Year's Kisses": a) *Wake Up and Live* b) *On the Avenue*, or c) *Every Night At Eight*?

2. In which movie was she required to contend with *two* Don Ameches: a) *That Night in Rio* b) *Weekend in Havana* or c) *The Great American Broadcast*?

3. Alice Faye's most frequent co-star was a) Tyrone Power b) Don Ameche or c) John Payne?

Bing Crosby: The durable crooner with the trade-marked easy-going style may have ventured into purely dramatic roles, but he will be best remembered as the light-hearted star of a score of light-headed musicals.

1. Name the musicals in which Bing co-starred with a) Marion Davies b) W. C. Fields, and c) Beatrice Lillie.

2. Can you name the four musicals with Bing Crosby in which the word "rhythm" appears in the title?

3. In which musical movie did Bing sing a) "I've Got a Pocketful of Dreams" b) "Abraham", and c) "Let's Bake a Sunshine Cake?"

Judy Garland: What can be said about this gifted singer that has not already been said? At her remarkable best, she made the screen glow, and one view of her in *Meet Me in St. Louis*, tremulously singing about "The Boy Next Door," is probably worth more than all the printed testimonials to her talent.

1. She was never better than when she sang about un-requited love. In which movie did she sing a) "But Not For Me" b) "Better Luck Next Time," and c) "The Man That Got Away"?

2. In which films did she appear in roles first played by a) Lynn Fontanne b) Janet Gaynor, and c) Margaret Sullavan?

3. One of the "Mickey-Judy" musicals ends with a patriotic salute to "God's Country." Was it a) *Babes in Arms*, b) *Babes on Broadway*, c) *Strike Up the Band*?

Fred Astaire: The Master of the Movie Musical, the man with the winged feet, and perhaps the one male musical star who can truly be called a joy forever.

1. In which musicals with Ginger Rogers was he a) amused to discover that she was pretending to be a Countess b) obliged to pretend that she could teach *him* how to dance, and c) bewildered by his feelings about her as his psychiatric patient?

2. Name his dancing partner in each of the following musical numbers—and the movie in which they performed it: a) "My Shining Hour" b) "Mr. and Mrs. Hoofer at Home", and c) "He Loves and She Loves".

3. Astaire's numbers were often self-contained dramatic pieces. In which numbers—and in which films—did he play a) a gambler bent on suicide b) a jewel thief, and c) a tough detective?

Betty Grable: The Pin-Up Queen of the forties, she cheer-fully admitted her deficiencies in singing and acting, but it didn't matter: her well-rounded figure, her engaging directness, and her brightly Technicolored movies, made her an adornment of her era.

1. In which movie did she sing, "If you're romantic, chum, pack up your duds and come to Acapulco"? Was it a) *Pin-Up Girl* b) *Springtime in the Rockies*, or c) *Billy Rose's Diamond Horseshoe*?

2. Grable appeared in a remake of her 1943 musical, *Coney Island*. Was it called a) *Meet Me After the Show* b) *Wabash Avenue*, or c) *My Blue Heaven*?

3. Name the Grable movies in which she played roles played earlier by a) Janet Gaynor b) Jean Arthur and c) Carole Lombard.

Gene Kelly: The song-and-dance man with the jaunty air, infectious grin, and irrepressible feet, the happy dancer-in-the-rain who made our spirits soar.

1. Kelly has always enjoyed using props imaginatively in his dances. In which movies did he work with a) a mop b) a newspaper, and c) a mouse?

2. With which partners did he a) leap across the Scot-tish highlands b) cavort to a tune about Moses, and c) sing Cole Porter's "You're Just Too Too"?

3. Which of the following Gershwin songs was *not* heard in *An American in Paris*: a) "By Strauss" b) "Love Walked In" c) "S'Wonderful", or d) "Tra-La-La-La"?

Jeanette MacDonald: Before there was the "Iron Butterfly" of her films with Nelson Eddy, there was the charming and piquant lady who co-starred in a group of tuneful operettas. But her place in film history is un-deniable.

1. She made four movies with Maurice Chevalier. In which one did she sing Rodgers and Hart's "Isn't It

Romantic?"

2. Name the MacDonald-Eddy films in which she played a) an opera star whose brother escapes from prison b) the mistress of a mining camp bar who falls for an outlaw, and c) the co-star (with her husband) of a long-running Broadway musical.

3. Which of the following actors never appeared in a film with Miss MacDonald: Spencer Tracy, Robert Young, Robert Taylor, or Lew Ayres?

Dan Dailey: Never a superstar, he managed to be ingratiating in a number of musicals as a loose-limbed and often loose-living song-and-dance man.

1. His favorite co-star was Betty Grable. In which of their films together was he a) the father of Mona Freeman and Connie Marshall b) the television-star husband of Grable, both of whom pined for a baby, and c) an alcoholic entertainer on the skids?

2. Dailey's best song-and-dance number was probably "Situation Wise," in which he drunkenly parodied Madison Avenue advertising lingo. In which musical movie did this number appear?

3. In which movie did he play Donald O'Connor's father?

(Answers on page 156)

These kids have talent. Fred Astaire and Judy Garland in their infectious "Couple of Swells" number from EASTER PARADE (1948)

TOGETHER AGAIN FOR THE FIRST TIME

Now pay attention. Each item below describes two roles in different films. Identify the movies and the players. Then name at least one movie in which the two performers co-starred.

1. A fugitive murderer named Glenn, holding the Hiliard family at bay/Helen Miller, wife to the popular bandleader named Glenn

2. Big John McMasters, friend of Square John Sand/Grace Kahn, wife to the popular songwriter named Gus

3. Violinist Paul Boray, lover of rich, alcoholic Helen Wright/Constance MacKenzie, mother of Allison

4. Sara Muller, wife to underground patriot Kurt Muller/A homicidal handyman named Danny

5. Famous defense attorney Matthew Drummond/Stage star Charlotte Inwood

6. Quaker father Jess Birdwell at the time of the Civil War/Wealthy, promiscuous Mrs. Vera Simpson

7. Dancing star Jerry Travers/Alvin York's loving girlfriend Gracie

8. Troubled Shakespearean star Anthony John/Janie, a girl confused by three ardent beaus

9. Scheming, ambitious business tycoon Dan Packard/Milly, wife to Adam and his many brothers

10. Sinister Gregory Anton, bent on driving his wife insane/Mary Matthews, wife to presidential candidate Grant Matthews

11. Gangster Rocky Sullivan, friend of Father Jerry/Katherine Grant, girlfriend of Joe Wilson, who has been jailed on a false charge and threatened with mob violence.

12. Heiress Ellen Andrews/Cowboy Rooster Cogburn

13. Charles Bovary, husband to Emma/Predatory, man-chasing perfume salesgirl Crystal Allen

14. Dashing, heroic Captain Geoffrey Vickers/Wicked, murderous Phyllis Dietrichson

15. Hard-bitten cowboy Gil Carter, helpless witness to a lynching/Seductive Marie, romantically tangling with fishing boat owner Morgan in wartime Martinique

16. Driven police detective Jim McLeod/Jaded Lady Brett Ashley, juggling admirers in a Spanish bullfighting town

17. Dr. Saperstein, tending to pregnant patient Rosemary Woodhouse (or is he?)/Beautiful, willful Elizabeth Bennet

18. Pope Julius II/Aging musical star Helen Lawson

19. Sardonic Andrew Wyke, author of detective fiction/Nicole Diver, neurotic, mercurial wife to Dick Diver

20. Snobbish social tyrant Elliott Templeton/Jean Maitland, cynical hoofer and resident at the Footlights Club

(Answers on page 157)

Bonus Photo Question:
Together for the first—and last—time: two of the screen's greatest stars, Greta Garbo and Clark Gable. Can you name the 1931 movie in which they appeared?

THE CHILDREN'S HOUR

Child actors on the screen can be either obnoxious and unnatural brats, born to be throttled, or remarkably talented and winning performers who can steal a movie from under the noses of their elders. Below is a group of characters played by well-known child actors who generally (but not always) fit into the latter category. How many of these talented tots can you identify?

1. Mary Tilford in *These Three* (1936)
2. Bill Peck in *Peck's Bad Boy* (1934)
3. Jody Baxter in *The Yearling* (1946)
4. Dinah Lord in *The Philadelphia Story* (1940)
5. Joey Starrett in *Shane* (1953)
6. Ulysses Macauley in *The Human Comedy* (1943).
7. Dan in *Captains Courageous* (1937)
8. Mytyl in *The Blue Bird* (1940)
9. The title role in *Oliver!* (1968)
10. Penny Craig in *Three Smart Girls* (1936)

11. Jim Hawkins in *Treasure Island* (1950)
12. Emil Bruckner in *Tomorrow the World* (1944)
13. Helen Keller in *The Miracle Worker* (1962)
14. Tootie Smith in *Meet Me in St. Louis* (1944)
15. Donald Martin in *Anchors Aweigh* (1945)
16. Huw Morgan in *How Green Was My Valley* (1941)
17. Rhoda Penmark in *The Bad Seed* (1956)
18. David Balfour in *Kidnapped* (1938)
19. Francie Nolan in *A Tree Grows in Brooklyn* (1945)
20. Jane Banks in *Mary Poppins* (1964)

(Answers on page 157)

Bonus Photo Question:
In BLONDIE IN SOCIETY (1941), one of the many "Blondie" features from the popular comic strip, Dagwood (Arthur Lake) prepares to run for his bus, with Blondie (Penny Singleton), Baby Dumpling and dog Daisy in assistance. (No doubt he'll knock over mailman Irving Bacon.) Question: who played Baby Dumpling, later known more appropriately as Alexander?

BLACK STAR

The following characters, all black, played important roles in the films in which they appeared. Name the actor or actress who played each role, and the movie in which he/she figured. (We've supplied a hint with each name.)

1. Lucas Beauchamp (on trial for murder)

2. Lena Younger ("In my mother's house, there is God!")

3. Delilah Johnson ("I jes' wanna *do* for you, Miss Bea.")

4. Digger Ed Jones (partner to Coffin Ed Johnson)

5. Homer Smith ("A-*men!*")

6. Nathan Lee Morgan (proud husband to Rebecca)

7. Prissy ("I don't know nothin' 'bout birthin' babies!")

8. Thackeray (a lesson for the Cockney toughs)

9. Berenice Sadie Brown (friend to Frankie and John Henry)

10. Jack Jefferson (his mistress: Eleanor)

11. Tom Robinson (defended by Atticus Finch)

12. Noah ("I shoulda seen de glory!")

13. Brutus Jones ("The drums! The drums!")

14. Joe (Queenie's husband, "scared o' dyin'" [two actors])

15. Petunia Jackson ("Takin' a chance on love")

(Answers on page 158)

Bonus Photo Question:
In this scene from GEORGE WASHINGTON SLEPT HERE (1942), Jack Benny and Ann Sheridan confront their highly reluctant maid, played by one of the best black actresses—and the only one to win an Academy Award. Her name?

DICK POWELL:
Renaissance Man of the Movies

By Tony Thomas

It's interesting to speculate how Dick Powell would have felt about the huge wave of nostalgia which rose in the mid-sixties and dredged up his image as a glossy young crooner. He and Ruby Keeler were sometimes invited to showings of their Warner musicals at film societies and kidded each other about the pleasant absurdity of it all. But Powell died a few years before the Busby Berkeley craze reached epidemic proportions and focussed glaring attention on these antique, unique musical fantasies. Powell was a man with a strong ego and a genuine feeling for the spotlight, but he may not have liked the emphasis on a phase of his career at which he rebelled. Few actors in Hollywood tried as hard, and succeeded so completely, in changing an image. He came to specialize in playing flippant tough guys and in the last ten years of his life rose to become one of the industry's top television producers. The Warner Bros. image was so far out of line with what Powell was in real life, especially in his later years, that it might have been that of another man.

There is a cult regard for the picture in which he made his transition from crooner to tough guy: the 1945 RKO production of *Murder, My Sweet*, recently remade under the original Raymond Chandler title of *Farewell, My Lovely*. But it would be worthwhile to stage a Powell retrospective of some of the other films that followed: *Cornered* (1945), *Johnny O'Clock* (1947), *To the Ends of the Earth* (1948), *Pitfall* (1948), *Station West* (1948), *Mrs. Mike* (1950) and *The Tall Target* (1951). The likelihood of such a retrospective is remote since none of the films is unusual in scope or subject matter. But what a viewing of these pictures reveals is a sure-footed movie actor, entirely in command of his presence and never less than believable. Powell was not a gifted interpretive actor and he never extended himself. He simply knew the range of his ability and played his material head-on. He was an absolutely confident man, and the sense of authority that marked his acting in the later stages of his career was even more apparent in his business life. David Niven and Charles Boyer were his partners in owning and operating Four Star Television, but it was Powell who ran the show and made the company one of the most successful of the day. Suffice to say that when Powell died, so did Four Star.

Powell was born in a small town in Arkansas in November of 1904 and grew up in Little Rock. He was one of three brothers who all did well in business. Brother

FLIRTATION WALK (1934). With Ruby Keeler

MODEL WIFE (1941). With Joan Blondell

Howard ended his career as the vice president of the Illinois Central Railroad. He and Dick were active choir-boys; in fact they were more than active—they were organized. They sang solo and duet, and worked all the denominations in rotation. Powell recalled his days as a boy soprano: "I sang every Sunday morning at the Episcopal church, where my family were parishioners but I also sang in the Presbyterian church in the evening, at the Masonic Lodge on Wednesday night and at the Jewish synagogue on Friday night. I was so busy I could have used MCA to represent me in those days. After I got out of high school and finished two years at Little Rock College—working my way through as a soda jerker, a telephone company order-taker and a grocery clerk, I joined the Royal Peacock Orchestra in Louisville, Kentucky, and got my start in show business, which is what I'd always wanted."

In his early days he was billed as Richard E. (for Ewing) Powell, Tenor, and sang semi-classics in what he confessed to be a "high, whining voice." Even at that time Powell had an instinct for spotting trends in public taste—an instinct that would eventually make him a millionaire—and he decided to change not only his singing style but to supplement it with performances on the banjo. As a pop-singer-banjo player, he landed with the Charlie Davis band and traveled with them through the mid-West, with their appearances at dance halls and movie theatres. Spotting another opportunity, Powell opted for becoming a master of ceremonies at the Indiana Theatre in Indianapolis, then graduating to the Stanley Theatre in Pittsburgh, which would prove to be his

94

springboard to the Big Time. A Warner Bros. talent scout arranged a contract for him in 1932. It was somewhere in this period of his life that Powell married for the first time, although it was a short-lived marriage. The first Mrs. Dick Powell discovered, as did Joan Blondell and June Allyson, that though her husband was an invariably charming and affable fellow, his mind was more often than not fixed on business opportunities and deals.

By the time Powell appeared in his first picture, Warners' *Blessed Event* in 1932, he was a well-rounded entertainer, having sung under all kinds of conditions, played a variety of musical instruments and introduced a multitude of acts as an MC. In the first half dozen years of his film career he was stuck with a juvenile image. Looking much younger than he actually was, he found himself locked into insipid screenplays, largely as a callow crooner. Once Powell was clear of his seven-year contract with Warners, he never went back to the studio and seldom spoke with any fondness of the period. He was not only a victim of rigid type casting but his own sense of business acumen clashed with the notorious tightness of the brothers Warner. He was first signed at a wage of $500 a week, which was half of what he earned as an MC at the Stanley Theatre. After three months of inactivity, Warners cut him down to $300 a week and at the time he appeared in *42nd Street*, he was getting only $98. Powell, who had a love of making money, never forgave Warners. He made two dozen musicals at Warners and became their biggest musical draw but he never received what he thought he was worth. In 1937 Powell was one of the top ten box office stars but his stock declined swiftly thereafter, so much so that when he left the studio in early 1939 he was unable to arrange any really lucrative deals.

Dick Powell's problem at this time was not financial—he had already made investments in land and property—but the much more serious one of professional standing. It also bothered him that an actor at that point in Hollywood history had almost no say in production. Many of his friends claim that his primary talent was that of an executive. Looking back on his leaving Warners, he said, "I had learned two things. I knew I wasn't the greatest singer in the world, and I saw no reason why an actor should restrict himself to any one particular phase of the business." Eager to prove himself in a milieu other than musical, Powell jumped at the chance to appear in one of the first of the piquant Preston Sturges comedies, *Christmas in July* (1940), and the results were enough for the industry to at least take a little notice, although more of Sturges than of Powell. He followed this film with two marital comedies co-starring his wife Joan Blondell, *I Want a Divorce* (1940) and *Model Wife* (1944), the titles of both being more than pungent since their actual marriage was limping to an end. Neither picture did well and the best that Powell could then get was playing second lead in Abbott and Costello's *In the Navy*, the sort of part that threw him back almost a decade.

Powell remained tenacious. He accepted a contract with Paramount, on the understanding that he would get a variety of roles. Instead it was a case of one lightweight musical after another, resulting in much impatience on the part of Powell: "They bought a story I liked and I asked if I could do it. It was *Double Indemnity*. They wouldn't give it to me and assigned me instead to *Bring on the Girls*. This was the end of the road for me, so I refused to do it and they suspended me. This went on for ten or twelve weeks. One day, in an elevator, I ran into Frank Freeman, then head of Paramount's production. I said, 'Frank, this is silly. I'm not going to do this kind of picture any more. I don't like them, and you might as well let me out.' And he did. I then went over to RKO and told them my little tale of woe."

Powell's timing at this point was exceptionally good: "It so happened they had bought Raymond Chandler's *Farewell, My Lovely*. They gave me the script, I read it and said I'd do it. The director, Edward Dmytryk, didn't want me because my box office appeal was down to zero and he couldn't think of me as anything but the singing marine. But I begged so hard for the part that he finally took a chance on me. It was a big success and started me all over again as the new, tough Powell."

Powell admitted that he sensed a new trend in movie acting and took this as an opportunity to get in on it. His Philip Marlowe was tough and cynical but also a little elegant and polished in his speech and manner. His voice was a great asset; the tenor tones had settled into a smooth baritone and his singing, which he now limited to radio, was more agreeable than before. The singing background was valuable because it enabled him to pitch his speaking voice accurately and if, as most actors believe, acting is fifty per cent voice, Powell was well aware of it. His well-modulated voice and smooth diction brought him all the radio work he could handle. As a musical star he appeared almost weekly throughout his singing days, but with the new image he starred as a private eye on radio, first as *Richard Rogue* and then, for several years, as *Richard Diamond, Private Detective*.

In these busy years, there were never enough hours in the day for all the things Dick Powell wanted to do. Joan Blondell had divorced him, presumably because he devoted litttle time to family life, and in 1945 he married MGM starlet June Allyson, nineteen years his junior. In time she would make similar charges. In 1950 they appeared in two MGM pictures together, *The Reformer and the Redhead* and *Right Cross* but by then he was already looking around for fresh fields to conquer. He took his first crack at being a director in 1953 with *Split Second*, which was far from a box-office bonanza but proved that he knew what to do behind the cameras. Three years would lapse before he directed another, the John Wayne Mongolian Western *The Conqueror*, which he also produced. In the interim he had established himself in television, sensing that was where Hollywood's future lay. In this view he was almost alone. Powell was the first major movie star to embrace the new outlet, and not simply as a performer but as a producer.

Remembering this early television period, he said, "I looked around and saw that the movie business was going badly. All the studios had dropped their contract players and it was getting tougher and tougher to make a buck. I had been fascinated by the new medium ever since we began to get network shows in California and I figured that this was the time to break in on the wrestling and the comedy shows with good Hollywood drama. I got together with my friends Charles Boyer, Rosalind Russell and Joel McCrea and we planned a show to be called *Four Star Playhouse*. But Roz and Joel took one look at themselves in the kinescopes and said, 'This stuff will never make it. Besides the work is too hard.' So they backed out. I finally rounded up David Niven and I went to New York to try and sell the show with only three stars. I was lucky. I ran into a man named Nat Wolf, who was the new head of television programming for a big advertising agency. Nat had worked for me as the director of my old radio show *Richard Diamond* and he owed me a favor because I had released him from the contract so he could take the agency job. He sold our show to the Singer Sewing Machine Company and we were on our way."

MURDER, MY SWEET (1944). With Claire Trevor

Four Star Playhouse gradually begot offspring, until by the end of the fifties the company was one of the most productive houses in Hollywood. There were times when they had half a dozen series running concurrently on several networks. The success made Powell a great many friends but also a few detractors who felt that he used his rather glib and ingratiating manner to sell products that might have had a harder time otherwise. Powell made his last appearance in a feature film in 1954, *Susan Slept Here*, then happily opted for limiting his acting to television, while at the same time advancing himself in the film business as a producer-director. Powell was so winning in these days that Howard Hughes offered him the post of managing director of the ailing RKO studios, which Powell turned down. Instead he accepted a contract from Twentieth Century-Fox, for whom he ended up making only two films—*The Enemy Below* (1957), by far his most distinguished work as a film maker, and *The Hunters* (1958). He finally left Fox after several ambitious projects failed to materialize. To Powell time was money and not to be squandered.

Powell was never pretentious about anything he did. Some people found him somewhat self-satisfied and even a little smug but these are not unusual characteristics in a man with an apparent midas touch. On the whole his many friends claim he was invariably pleasant and for a man as busy as he was, he was easily approachable and seemed to find time for everyone and everything. About his work as a director he made no lofty claims. "I do the best I can with the type of material I am able to get. I have no illusions about joining the company of Willie Wyler, Billy Wilder, Henry Koster, Elia Kazan, John Huston, Carol Reed and the very remarkable John Ford. I admire all those men for the honesty with which they attempt to do their pictures." Powell claimed that the only difference in making films for television and for the theatre derives from the size of the screen; that the former should be less elaborate than the latter and more intimate—that effectiveness is lost in television if there is too much going on.

Politically Powell was conservative, a classic example of the self-made man with a passion for work and a rather simplistic attitude that anyone can do what he wants if he tries hard enough. Certainly for him it worked. Those who worked for him also worked hard, and he expected proficiency. It was his belief that the unions did not contribute much to the raising of work standards throughout the film industry and that all the progress was the result of hard-working individuals. In running Four Star, his concern was finding talent: "The main problem in filmaking today is the same as before—there isn't enough real talent. There are not enough great actors, great writers or great directors. This lack of talent caused the death of live television. I know of only half a dozen writers capable of writing film scripts that don't have to be re-written and re-written. I'm using the word talent in its fullest sense, and believe me, there isn't enough of it." He felt that

more and more actors would become involved in the business side of the profession. "The income tax has changed the oldtime movie star from an exciting, careless, colorful individual into a business man. He's got to be a business man. If he isn't he can't survive, no matter what his earning capacity may be."

It was Powell's intention to develop Four Star into the biggest possible production house and to move into feature film making. But a completely unexpected factor turned that ambition into an unfulfilled dream. Early in 1962 it was found that Powell had cancer, and in an advanced stage. He took treatments and soon claimed that the disease had been arrested, even calling a press conference to announce his confidence. It was characteristic of Powell that he fully believed himself above it all, and he kept up his constant round of activities. The previous year he and June Allyson had decided on a divorce, with a settlement so large she could have started a rival company. But with the invasion of cancer they changed their minds, and she stayed with him. On November 14, 1962, Powell passed his fifty-eighth birthday and by then he was no longer openly discussing his cancer. He probably believed that he would survive but in fact he had less than two months to live. He resigned as managing director of Four Star and took the position of Chairman of the Board, continuing to go to his office at the studio—the studio that was once Republic and would later become CBS Cinema Center. He continued to advise on production and to answer his correspondence to within the last three weeks. Then his strength swiftly ebbed and on the evening of January 3, 1963, with June holding his hand, Dick Powell quietly died.

TO THE ENDS OF THE EARTH (1948). With Signe Hasso

THE MOVIE DETECTIVES

Many popular fictional detectives found their way to the screen in the thirties and forties, usually in a series of movies with low (if not miniscule) budgets and a cast of contract players who had enthusiasm but not much talent. Nobody minded, least of all the regular moviegoers who enjoyed the fast action and sometimes tricky plots.

In this quiz, we've trotted out a batch of these movie detectives and asked you to identify them, and the actors who played them.

The first photographs involve three of the many screen incarnations of the sharp-minded but occasionally exasperating detective created by S. S. Van Dine. Name this detective, and, in each case, the actor hard at work solving the murders.

(Answers on page 158)

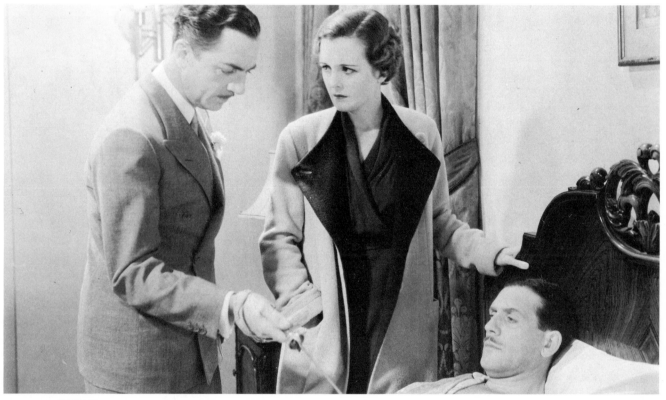

Photo 1
The year: 1933. The mystery: THE KENNEL MURDER CASE. The lady: Mary Astor. The gentleman in bed: Paul Cavanagh.

Photo 2
A year later, in THE DRAGON MURDER CASE, the great detective (extreme left) gathers the suspects together.

Photo 3
In 1935, the detective had a rather unlikely interpreter in this actor. On either side: Rosalind Russell and Louise Fazenda. The movie is THE CASINO MURDER CASE.

Photo 4
The courtroom setting would lead you to believe that Erle Stanley Gardner's popular defense attorney is on the job again. You're right. Here he is in THE CASE OF THE HOWLING DOG (1934), with Dorothy Tree and Mary Astor. Name the attorney and the actor. (Yes, he certainly got around.)

Photo 5
On the trail of an arch-villain, this detective was the extremely popular creation of Chester Gould. He was the hero of many feature films and a few serials. To reveal this movie's title is to reveal all. Can you name the detective and the actor who played him? (The actress at the controls is young Phyllis Isley, later and better known as Jennifer Jones.)

Photo 6
The fellow in the hat was the hero of a series of low-budget mysteries of the forties. As an ex-thief who moved to the right side of the law, he hunted down criminals in his own raffish, offhand way. What was his name, and who played the role? (The others are George E. Stone, Lynn Merrick, and an unidentified tot.)

Photo 7
In this scene from BLONDES AT WORK (1938), Betty Compson holds a gun on Glenda Farrell. Ms. Farrell was playing the intrepid, wise-cracking reporter-sleuth that she, Lola Lane, and Jane Wyman all handled in a series of low-budget Warners movies. Can you name this lady?

Photo 8
One of the best known of all fictional detectives was played by the actor at the right in a Columbia series that began in 1940. Who was the detective and the actor? (In this 1941 scene: James Burke, Ann Doran, and Margaret Lindsay as secretary and sidekick Nikki Porter.)

Photo 9
The gentleman at the left was named Robert Ordway, but he was better known by another name in a series of cheaply made mysteries starting in 1943. He was a crime-solver who used psychological methods in his work. Here, in THE MILLERSON CASE (1947), he examines a hole in his hat with Addison Richards. What was his popular name, and who played the role?

Photo 10
The debonair actor in the hat at the center of this photograph is playing Leslie Charteris' equally debonair detective in a 1940 movie. He played the role several times in a mediocre series. Name the actor and the detective (both his true name and the name by which he is known). (Side note: the actor on his left is none other than Bela "Dracula" Lugosi.)

Photo 11
An equally suave detective of the forties was Michael Arlen's "Falcon." The Falcon was originally played by George Sanders, who decided to leave the series in 1942. He was replaced by his real-life brother, shown here at the right with Barbara Hale and Sheldon Leonard in THE FALCON IN HOLLYWOOD (1944). Name this actor.

Photo 12
Starting in 1938, Warner Bros. filmed a series of mystery programmers revolving about Carolyn Keene's teenaged detective, Nancy Drew. Here she is in NANCY DREW AND THE HIDDEN STAIRCASE (1939), with dad John Litel and sidekick Frankie Thomas. Can you name the actress who played Nancy?

Photo 13 (Answers on page 158)
The greatest of all fictional detectives is probably Sherlock Holmes, and he was played with finesse and style by Basil Rathbone in a series of neatly wrought thrillers. Nigel Bruce was equally marvelous as loyal, bumbling Dr. Watson. Since Ida Lupino (below) only appeared in one of the Holmes movies, you are asked to name that film.

INTERMISSION

ECHOES FROM THE
EARLY YEARS OF SOUND

One of the least explored yet most fascinating periods in film history encompasses the years in which movies were first learning to talk. Many films stiffly imitated stage techniques; others used sound sparingly or awkwardly. Yet many interesting and even impressive films were made. At the same time, while a number of unfortunate players were finding their careers demolished, others were just beginning to learn their craft and to take that long, steep climb to stardom.

It was an exhilarating, exasperating, and (for many) painful time. Genres and sub-genres surfaced to popularity, then sank out of sight. A parade of snarling gangsters, fallen women, straying husbands, and ambitious chorines marched across the screen, occasionally into immortality, mostly into oblivion.

Here are some items about movies of that period, and the personalities who were part of it.

Two familiar features of the early sound years were one-word titles suggesting sordid activities and victimized women who were suspected of indulging in those activities. In *Compromised* (1931), poor Rose Hobart was a pitiful slavey who marries drunkard Ben Lyon, then almost loses him to society girl Juliette Compton. *Illicit* (1931) actually found Barbara Stanwyck living with James Rennie without benefit of marriage and quarreling only *after* they tie the knot. In *Wicked* (1931), put-upon Elissa Landi was a pregnant mother sentenced to prison for accidentally killing a detective. And Constance Bennett, who was repeatedly playing women-no-better-than-they-should-be in the early sound years, starred in a 1931 curiosity called *Bought*, as the illegitimate daugher of her true-life father, Richard Bennett. Although 1931 was clearly a banner year for movies devoted to fallen ladies, there were others before and after: *Outcast* (Corinne Griffith) in 1928, *Framed* (Evelyn Brent) in 1930, and *Shopworn* (Barbara Stanwyck) in 1932, are merely three of many. One 1930 movie, reversing the trend, was called *Not Damaged*. There were also many movies with titillating *two*-word titles such as *Hot Heels* (1928), *Naughty Baby* (1929), *Hot Stuff* (1929), and *Tanned Legs* (1929).

*　　*　　*　　*

In 1931, a Columbia movie called *The Guilty Generation* had a curious resemblance to *The Godfather* of the

Two troubled ladies from the early sound years. Above: Barbara Stanwyck, with James Rennie, in ILLICIT (1931). Below: Constance Bennett, with Ray Milland, in BOUGHT (1931)

seventies. Leo Carrillo starred as Mike Palermo, a socially ambitious gangster who is concerned with protecting his offspring from the day's sordid realities. His bloody war with the Ricca family has disastrous results when his daughter Maria (Constance Cummings) inevitably falls in love with young Marco Ricca (Robert Young). Understandably, Maria postpones her wedding to Marco. ("Get married, and have a bomb planted in our wedding cake?'' she asks.) Guess who plays Robert Young's tough Chicago papa? None other than Boris Karloff, only three movies away from playing the Frankenstein monster.

*   *   *   *

Several years before playing Chinese detective Charlie Chan, Swedish actor Warner Oland played an Oriental figure of an entirely different stripe: the insidious, diabolical Dr. Fu Manchu. In *The Mysterious Dr. Fu Manchu* (1929), under Rowland V. Lee's direction, he was the menace supreme, plotting to push hero Neil Hamilton into quicklime, or hypnotizing his innocent ward, young Jean Arthur. O. P. Heggie was on hand as Nayland Smith of Scotland Yard, who succeeds in foiling Fu Manchu. The film's props included trapdoors, cut telephone wires, peepholes, and poisoned darts. A year later, the same principal players starred in *The Return of Dr. Fu Manchu* (1930, also released as *The New Adventures of Dr. Fu Manchu*). In this sequel, the doctor is apparently resurrected after what would seem to be a definitive

Warner Oland menaces Neil Hamilton and Jean Arthur in THE RETURN OF DR. FU MANCHU (1930)

death. (He is thrown over a balcony edge into a pool with a bomb in his hand that explodes as he hits the water!)

* * * *

Question: what role was played by Walter Huston, Jack Oakie, and Joe E. Brown? Answer: Elmer Kane, the egotistical small-town boy who becomes a baseball hero despite himself. Walter Huston starred in *Elmer the Great*, the original stage version written by Ring Lardner and George M. Cohan in 1928. The following year, Jack Oakie appeared in a film version, now called *Fast Company*. Directed by A. Edward Sutherland, it also featured Evelyn Brent, Richard ("Skeets") Gallagher, and Gwen Lee as an empty-headed friend of the heroine's, who "was fired from her job at the Five-and-Ten because she didn't know the prices." In 1933, Joe E. Brown played Elmer in *Elmer the Great*, under Mervyn LeRoy's direction. Patricia Ellis was the heroine, and Frank McHugh was featured as a character endearingly called High Hips Healy.

* * * *

A dozen years before Hedy Lamarr made movie history (of sorts) by intoning the line "I am Tondelayo" in MGM's *White Cargo*, an early sound version of Leon Gordon's play had turned up on the screen. A 1930 British movie that required the services of two directors—J.B. Williams and A.W. Barnes—this *White Cargo* starred as the half-caste wanton an actress whose name was as improbable and as fraught with meaning as Theda Bara's. She was called Gypsy Rhouma, and, perhaps to spare us all from the punsters, this was her one and only film. Also in the cast were two budding young English actors named Maurice Evans and Tom Helmore.

* * * *

Director Dorothy Arzner, whose work is now being re-evaluated, shared a directorial credit with Robert Milton on an early 1930 movie called *Behind the Makeup*. The film starred William Powell in another of the villainous characterizations he gave throughout the silent years and into the thirties, before he embodied the debonair Nick Charles. Powell, displaying an Italian accent and even speaking lines in Italian, was a cad who steals comedian Hal Skelly's act and girlfriend (Fay Wray), before ending an ignominious suicide. Others in the cast were suave Paul Lukas and Kay Francis as an adventuress with a penchant for gambling.

* * * *

In the early sound years, until they wore out their welcome, musicals were extremely popular movie fare. Most of them were hastily assembled revues with sketchy plots that frequently came to a halt for musical numbers.

But they were a novelty, and audiences and even some critics enjoyed them. One called *The New Movietone Follies of 1930* was praised by *The New York Times* as "a smartly produced, wise-cracking affair" which "achieved its purpose in creating gusts of laughter." Its non-name cast included El Brendel, Marjorie White, Frank Richardson, and Noel Francis, but the song titles were pleasantly evocative of the period: "I'd Love to Be a Talking Picture Queen," "I'm Bashful," and "I Feel a Certain Feeling Coming On."

* * * *

Paul Muni made his screen debut as a doomed prisoner in *The Valiant* (1929). He received favorable notices but his role in a second film, *Seven Faces* (1929), was more challenging, and certainly much stranger than the first. Under Berthold Viertel's direction, he played Papa Chibou, the lovable if slightly daft watchman at a Paris waxworks, who believes that all the wax figures are possessed souls. When the figures are to be sold at an auction, he steals his favorite, Napoleon. It hardly comes as a shock when he is arrested while carrying the figure through the streets. All ends well for dear Papa Chibou and he even helps to reunite two star-crossed lovers. The supporting cast included Marguerite Churchill, Russell Gleason, and the splendidly named Gustav von Seyffertitz.

* * * *

Can you conceive of a single movie starring Laurence Olivier, Erich von Stroheim, and Hugh Herbert? RKO-Radio Pictures did, and in 1931 the studio produced *Friends and Lovers*, a romantic drama concerning two English officers (Olivier and Adolphe Menjou) who fight for the love of a married woman (Lily Damita). The lady's husband, a nasty sort who enjoys whipping his wife, was played, not surprisingly, by Erich von Stroheim. After he is conveniently killed, the officers continue their feud, even to the Indian frontier. Hugh Herbert was present to relieve the tedium, and the movie was directed by Victor Schertzinger, who later ranged from the trills of Grace Moore (*One Night of Love, Love Me Forever*) to the slapstick of Hope and Crosby (*Road to Singapore, Road to Zanzibar*).

* * * *

In these first sound years, many venerable and sober-minded stories were newly adapted to the screen and given inappropriate and usually titillating titles. Thus, *Diversion*, a play by John Van Druten, was retitled *The Careless Age* (1929) to hint at the permissive behavior of the jazz era. A modern reworking of *East Lynne*, the perennial melodrama, was called *Ex-Flame* (1930). Booth Tarkington's story, "The Flirt," became *Bad Sister*

(1931). And William Vaughn Moody's play, *The Great Divide*, about a desperado in the Old West, was re-named *Woman Hungry*. (One half-expected to see *Rebecca of Sunnybrook Farm* remade as *Sinners in the Barnyard*.)

* * * *

Fun and games among the rowdy Marines was the subject of a 1930 farce called *Leathernecking*. Depicting life in the Marine Corps as a continual round of parties, yachting trips, and pillow fights, the movie would be of no consequence whatever except for its surprisingly strong credits. It was based on *Present Arms*, a musical play by Herbert Fields, Richard Rodgers, and Lorenz Hart, though it contained no songs. Its cast was headed by comedian Ken Murray as a private who impersonates an officer to impress his girl, Irene Dunne, in her film debut. Others contributing to the merriment were Ned Sparks, Eddie Foy, Jr., Louise Fazenda, and Lilyan Tashman. The director was Eddie Cline, who was to later face the supreme test of overseeing W. C. Fields in *My Little Chickadee, The Bank Dick*, and *Never Give a Sucker an Even Break*.

* * * *

Why Leave Home? was the question asked in a 1929 "audible" movie based on the play *The Cradle Snatchers*. Revolving about three neglected wives who get back at their wandering husbands by getting three callow youths to take them out, the film featured Sue Carol (later Mrs. Alan Ladd), cavorting as a chorus girl pursued by one of the husbands and executing some eye-popping gyrations to a song called "Doing the Boom Boom." The cast included Ilka Chase, Dixie Lee, Walter Catlett, and David Rollins. (*The Cradle Snatchers* had also been filmed under its original name two years earlier, under Howard Hawks' direction. In the early forties, it was adapted as a stage musical for Danny Kaye and retitled *Let's Face It*. The 1943 movie version of the musical starred Bob Hope and Betty Hutton.)

* * * *

A perennially popular film property over the years has been Ralph Spence's comedy melodrama, *The Gorilla*. Replete with all the trappings of its haunted-house sub-genre—sliding panels, trap doors, sudden shrieks, slapstick chases, etc.—it was initially filmed by First National in 1927, with Charles Murray, Alice Day, and Tully Marshall in the leading roles. Young Walter Pidgeon had a small role but in the 1931 remake he had a larger role in the proceedings. Edwin Maxwell, Lila Lee, and the legendary stuttering comic Joe Frisco (in his only thirties movie) had the leads. In 1939, Fox remade the story as a vehicle for its frenetic comedy team, the Ritz Brothers, with Bela Lugosi, Anita Louise, Patsy Kelly, and Lionel Atwill in support. (It is not reported who played the gorilla in any of the versions.)

* * * *

A 1929 audible musical called *Syncopation* trotted out the moth-eaten plot of the quarreling night club entertainers who are separated when the wife succumbs temporarily to a wealthy suitor. The movie was unremarkable, but it had an interesting cast, headed by Barbara Bennett, sister of Joan and Constance, in the first of three roles she played in the movies, and Robert Watson, who later made a small career out of playing Adolf Hitler. Featured roles were handled by Ian Hunter, Osgood Perkins (father of Anthony), Verree Teasdale, and singer Morton Downey in his first movie. Musical contributions were also made by Fred Waring and his Pennsylvanians.

A scene from LEATHERNECKING (1930), with Eddie Foy, Jr., Irene Dunne, and Ken Murray

William Wyler rehearses a scene for JEZEBEL (1938) with Bette Davis.

THREE:
"...AND WHO'S BEHIND THE CAMERA?"

Movie stars may glitter brightly, but a great many talented people devote their time to keeping these stars from crashing out of their orbits. These are the directors, photographers, special effects people, writers, designers, and musicians who combine their skills to make a movie work—and often keep it from falling apart.

In this section, we offer articles, quizzes and photographs involving these dedicated and hard-working men and women behind the camera.

The first article looks at several of our leading actors who turned in their greasepaint temporarily to become directors. Acts of daring, true, but their efforts had fascinating results . . .

ACTORS AS DIRECTORS

By Foster Hirsch

In much the same way that comedians often aspire to play Hamlet, actors frequently express the desire to direct. But with a few notable exceptions like Orson Welles, Laurence Olivier and Vittorio De Sica, few actors-turned-directors have been successful; and the history of film is littered with their failed attempts to prove themselves on the other side of the camera. The films are often interesting, however, because of their imperfections and because, frequently, they reflect the temperaments of the actors themselves.

Blighted, fragmented projects gain interest because we can often sense the colorful personalities of actors struggling behind the camera with an uncomfortable new role. *The Bigamist*, for instance, is a partially realized early fifties melodrama that nonetheless has the tough, no-nonsense quality of its actress-director, Ida Lupino. Filled with astute observations about the wayward husband and his two women, this grim, unpretentious film has a downbeat "B" movie aura that reflects Lupino's own hard-boiled style. Alan Arkin's *Little Murders* (1971) has the stinging comic edge that has marked the actor's performances; Arkin has coached the characters to sound like people in a hip blackout sketch, and the film has a Nichols and May cabaret style, cool, knowing, satirical. The characters take on Arkin's smug, ironic tone, carefully detaching themselves from Jules Feiffer's urban nightmare world. While the film is too self-conscious to be entirely successful, it is appealing in the same way that Arkin always is.

Sometimes, an actor's visual style is closely influenced by that of a director he has worked with. Thus, Clint Eastwood's *Play Misty for Me* (1972) shows clear signs of indebtedness to Don Siegel. The thriller has the cool, low-key sensuality of Eastwood's "Dirty Harry" character, and the same atmosphere of rot and corruption that pervades the big city backgrounds in many of Siegel's films. John Wayne's sloppy direction of *The Alamo* (1960) nonetheless reflects the actor's long association with John Ford; and, despite its sags, the film shares Ford's feeling for landscape and for pageantry as well as for patriotic American themes.

The work of actors turned directors is filled with curiosities and surprises. The films sometimes bear no relation to the actor's image or to the kinds of films that built his own career. Who, for instance, could have expected Cornel Wilde to be such an off-beat, provocative director? Wilde has produced a group of films with unusual themes and settings, and his work shows individuality and technical skill. His film on ecology, *No Blade of Grass* (1970), and his chase film, *The Naked Prey* (1966) have real energy and daring. Paul Newman is closely identified with cynical, unyielding characters like Hud and the Hustler and Cool Hand Luke, yet his three films—*Rachel, Rachel* (1968), *The Effect of Gamma Rays on Man-in-the-Moon Marigolds* (1972), and *Sometimes a Great Notion* (1972) are untypical of the movies that established his reputation. His two films with Joanne Woodward are domestic melodramas; they are sentimental woman's pictures with none of the hard edge or the bitter, sour tone that has dominated his own performances. The two films demonstrate a real feeling for the texture and rhythm of filmmaking. With their flashy editing techniques and their complex handling of space and time, the films declare a forthright infatuation with the process of filmmaking. Newman erases his own persona from the films and concentrates on the projects as spectacular vehicles for his wife. As the frustrated spinster schoolteacher in *Rachel, Rachel*, and as the embittered, tyrannical mother in *Marigolds*, Woodward gives her finest performances—Newman is acutely sensitive to his wife's abilities. Both films contain familiar elements —they are both mood pieces that depend on strong atmosphere—but they both seem fresh and genuine. Newman is a superb craftsman, and his beautifully controlled films have none of the frenzied, overwrought quality, none of the sense of doom or aborted intentions or wild overreaching, that often characterize the work of the actor as director.

Newman's films do not look like the work of an egocentric movie star drunk on power, and thus his projects don't have the idiosyncratic tone of a deeply per-

Paul Newman directing wife Joanne Woodward in RACHEL, RACHEL (1968)

sonal undertaking. His polished work doesn't have the intense, eccentric flavor of three of the most exhilarating films ever directed by actors: Charles Laughton's *Night of the Hunter* (1955), Marlon Brando's *One-Eyed Jacks* (1961), and Jack Nicholson's *Drive, He Said* (1971) are stunning, perverse achievements, clearly signed by actors with high-strung personalities and great personal style.

As actors, all three have often seemed to direct their own performances. They are each, of course, notorious scene-stealers, often unwilling to share the frame with fellow actors. Laughton, Brando, and Nicholson are egocentric, at times blatantly exhibitionistic performers for whom acting is a kind of virtuoso showing off. Unlike Nicholson, however, Laughton and Brando are compulsively experimental, infatuated with disguise and with transformations of their image. Both tried to escape typecasting, Brando refusing to play a series of hulking, inarticulate rebels, Laughton moving restlessly from drama to comedy and from menacing to likable characters. But both actors had career slumps during which, in threadbare scripts, they had nothing else to go on except star aura.

Nicholson, on the other hand, is much closer to the conventional notion of the Hollywood star, and we can say about him, in a way that does not apply to either Laughton or Brando, that he is always the same; he always seems to be playing himself. Brando and Laughton act; Nicholson behaves. In film after film, Nicholson is the modern anti-hero, a rebellious loner with a caustic sense of humor: audiences will always remember his humiliation of the waitress in *Five Easy Pieces* as a typical Nicholson moment. Grubby and laconic, Nicholson stands up against rigid authoritarians. Because he doesn't know how to follow the rules, he's forced to challenge narrow-minded establishment figures like Nurse Ratchet in *One Flew Over the Cuckoo's Nest*. With his loping gait, his easy sexuality, and his sharp wit, Nicholson woos the audience while not seeming to care whether the audience likes him or not. He has such a hip, winning persona that, even when he plays characters who are predominantly cynical (as in *Carnal Knowledge*) or foolish (as in *The Fortune*) or truly alienated (as in *The Passenger*), he looks like the hero, he charms the audience; and so he's a victim of his image in a way that Brando and Laughton are not.

It was inevitable that these three dominant, charismatic personalities would be drawn to directing; and it's significant that all three actors chose projects that in some way represent extensions of their star image and that contain thematic similarities to many of the films in which they have appeared. The results, predictably, are brilliant and stubborn, films that take risks in what they say and in how they say it. Though the three films have big studio budgets and (except for *Drive, He Said*) star performers, and though they each have genre trappings, they are at heart downbeat and experimental. *One-Eyed Jacks* is a

Marlon Brando directing ONE-EYED JACKS (1961)

Western, *The Night of the Hunter* is a horror film, *Drive, He Said* is a youth film, but they each defy genre conventions. Displaying their directors' unyielding temperaments, they are quirky and defiant films that belong to Andrew Sarris' category of "expressive esoterica." They were commercial failures at the time of their release, yet they have each developed underground reputations. New audiences respond to them favorably as dynamic reworkings of classic American genres.

One-Eyed Jacks and *Drive, He Said*, in particular, are acted very much in the styles of their famous directors. The performers sound like Brando and Nicholson, and so both films are overlaid with the directors' distinctively introspective temperaments; the films are shot through with a sullen, quicksilver moodiness, a charged sensuality. *One-Eyed Jacks* is the foremost Method Western, with the actors mimicking Brando's own tortuous verbal tics. The stylized interpretations escape parody, however; the halting, low-key delivery creates a volatile atmosphere that deepens the film's formula surfaces.

One-Eyed Jacks tells a routine Western story of revenge in which Rio (Marlon Brando) hunts down his former partner who has become a sheriff while Rio languished in prison. Before the showdown, Rio has a romance with the

111

Jack Nicholson directing DRIVE, HE SAID (1971)

The manneristic acting is matched by Brando's fresh visual treatment of the material: the story is set on the Monterey Peninsula, and the peculiar fir trees indigenous to the area, as well as the pounding surf, enclose the action in an eerie, almost mystical, framework. The lush scenery provides a startling substitute for the prairie and desert of traditional Westerns.

The deliberate, brooding quality of the acting is carried over into the pacing as well. Brando will not be hurried. He will not satisfy audience expectations. Eruptions of manic violence punctuate the story, as in the scenes of voluptuous masochism where Rio is brutalized by his enemy; but the bulk of the film is extravagantly slow-moving. Brando takes time for set pieces that embellish Rio's character, that provide mood and texture, but that do not advance the story. The film has a stately rhythm unusual in a Western. In pacing, visual concept, and performance, *One-Eyed Jacks* is a Grand Opera variation on the standard Western revenge drama.

Drive, He Said is tied to the subgenre of the youth film in much the same loose, free-form way that *One-Eyed Jacks* parallels the Western. With its campus setting and its politically and sexually hip characters, the film is iconographically related to the other youth culture films of the late sixties and early seventies. But Nicholson's film doesn't have the slick, hollow quality of its contemporaries; it doesn't have the extroverted, eager-to-please patina of *Getting Straight* or *The Magic Garden of Stanley Sweetheart* or *The Strawberry Statement*. As it opposes two kinds of students—one politically uncommitted, the other drawn deeper into psychosis in response to the madness of the times—the film maintains a wry, piercing tone that is surprisingly fresh. It is the most embittered of the anti-establishment films of the period, and the most original.

The lives of the two students—the basketball star and the dropped-out radical—are shrewdly cross-cut for thematic comparisons. In the film's political scheme, basketball represents the repressive world of dim-witted John Birchers, while the collapse of the radical movement is symbolized in the bizarre finale where the psychotic student releases snakes and lizards in a forbidding zoology lab.

Drive, He Said is brilliantly acted in a style of volcanic moodiness. As in Brando's film, the drama is contained in a series of charged confrontations in which the characters face each other warily, testing each other, jockeying for positions, as if poised for battle. The actors absorb Nicholson's own prickly, ironic persona, and they've picked up his mocking sensuality as well. William Tepper as the basketball player, Michael Margotta as the radical, Bruce Dern as the ferociously right-wing coach, and Karen Black as a teasing, adulterous, miserable faculty wife are dangerous and also strangely comical. They're knotty, complex individuals and yet they're also symbols, archetypes.

sheriff's stepdaughter. Narrative structure and characterization are standard for the genre, but Brando transforms the familiar motifs by constructing the film as a homage to his own legend. Under the guise of a conventional Western, he creates a self-scrutinizing study of his public persona that consists of equal parts of self-contempt and self-infatuation. Rio is a charming rogue, a skillful liar, a wanderer and vagabond who is nonetheless capable of acting honorably. Like most men of the West, he has a code, and he does what he has to do in order to satisfy it. Since he is both a scoundrel and a hero, the character is richly contradictory, and Brando plays him superbly, with a coiled intensity that suggests layers of neurotic conflict. He carefully coaxes the same level of seething intensity from the other actors: Pina Pellicer, as the stepdaughter; Karl Malden, as the sheriff; and Katy Jurado, as his wife. Confrontations are charged with varying degrees of menace with the result that *One-Eyed Jacks* is a dense psychological Western in which revenge and desire are enacted with primal urgency.

Nicholson's pacing is as deliberately lopsided as Brando's. The basketball scenes, with their savage view of cheerleaders and coaches and team spirit, are tautly edited, while other sequences reflect the hero's moody indecisiveness. The film swings wildly between low-key introspection and scenes of manic activity.

Charles Laughton, theatre-trained at the Royal Academy in London, was not a Method actor, and so it is not surprising that the tone of his film is very different from *One-Eyed Jacks* and *Drive, He Said*. *The Night of the Hunter* is not about an ambivalent sexy character who must define his concept of heroism. But the film is similar to the other two in starting with familiar genre elements—a hidden treasure, a chase, an evil preacher, two frightened children—and in transforming them through a heightened visual and acting style. Critics at the time regarded the film as an exercise in horror, and saw it as an extension of Laughton's own interest in playing sinister characters and in scaring audiences. But the film is much more than a horror movie, just as its methods are more complex than that of a standard realism with arty touches, as some contemporary reviewers were content to describe it.

With James Agee's fine script as a starting point, Laughton transforms a simple story, about children who flee from a homicidal preacher and end up in the custody of a woman who runs a home for orphans, into a parable of the struggle between good and evil, between innocence and worldliness. The story is told with extraordinary visual elegance; with its menacing shadows, its subtly stylized sets and its distortions of physical reality, *The Night of the Hunter* recalls the German expressionist films of the twenties. In American movies, there is nothing else that looks like it, except for certain baroque passages in the work of Orson Welles. The children's flight down river, for example, indicates the film's haunting visual imagination. The flight is presented not as a realistic chase, but as a fantasy with both lyrical and nightmarish elements: the severe, semi-abstract, high contrast compositions, the extreme close-ups of frogs that seem to both guard and threaten the children, the cross-cutting between the children and the preacher, who is photographed from a distance in silhouette against the stark horizon and the simple children's song that enriches the images. The sequence is at once terrifying and ineffably beautiful.

Again, as in *One-Eyed Jacks* and *Drive, He Said*, a decisive actor has obtained from his own actors performances that are uniform in style and excellence. Robert Mitchum's work as the cunning, reptilian preacher is surely his finest—he seems the incarnation of primordial evil. And he is matched by Lillian Gish's saintly country woman, a figure of transcendent virtue. Their final confrontation has the force of an archetypal encounter between good and evil.

The Night of the Hunter is one of the screen's great films, but because it didn't make money, because it was so off-beat and specialized, Laughton never got another chance to direct. Brando's on-set tantrums (he kept the crew waiting until the waves obtained the correct color and intensity) and his prima donna reputation will surely prevent his getting another directorial assignment. Only Nicholson, despite the commercial failure of his film, will perhaps be allowed a second chance. But the three films are distinguished achievements that prove that brilliant, innovative actors can also be inspired directors.

Charles Laughton, with Peter Graves and Billy Chapin, directing THE NIGHT OF THE HUNTER (1955)

THE MEN AT THE HELM

Here is a quiz built around the work of five of Hollywood's leading directors.

I. Otto Preminger

A. "In Love In Vain" was the hit song from which Otto Preminger-directed musical?

B. In which Preminger movie did Gene Tierney play a kleptomaniac?

C. True or false? Having struck out with Jean Seberg in *Saint Joan* in 1957, Preminger never used her again in a movie.

D. Who played the title role in Preminger's *Carmen Jones*?

E. Which one of the following movies from best-selling novels was *not* directed by Preminger: *Advise and Consent*, *The Cardinal*, or *Seven Days in May*?

II. Vincente Minnelli

A. Who played the title roles in *Yolanda and the Thief*?

B. Which Minnelli film had a key scene in which a distraught movie actress driving her car gives way to hysterics and almost crashes the car? And who played the actress?

C. True or false? In 1951, Minnelli won an Oscar for his direction of *An American in Paris*.

D. In which Minnelli movie did Lauren Bacall play a fashion director married to Gregory Peck?

E. Which of the following films was *not* directed by Minnelli: *The Long, Long Trailer*, *The Reluctant Debutante*, *Please Don't Eat the Daisies*, or *The Courtship of Eddie's Father*?

III. William Wellman

A. William Wellman's first major sound film was which of the following: *Little Caesar*, *The Public Enemy*, *G-Men*, or *I Was a Fugitive from a Chain Gang*?

B. Name the movie in which Wellman directed Barbara Stanwyck as a woman who ages from 16 to 109. Also name the movie in which he directed her as a stripper.

C. One of Wellman's classic films featured veteran Jane Darwell in an uncharacteristic role as a rowdy, cackling, bloodthirsty old harridan. Name this film.

D. From the following group of actors, select those who appeared in the cast of Wellman's *Battleground*: George Murphy, Lloyd Nolan, Brian Donlevy, James Whitmore, Richard Jaeckel.

E. In the fifties, Wellman made three movies with John Wayne. In which movie did Wayne sail an antique ferryboat through the Formosa Straits in wartime?

IV. Billy Wilder

A. True or false? Billy Wilder has won three Academy Awards for direction: for *The Lost Weekend*, *Sunset Boulevard*, and *The Apartment*.

B. In two successive years, Wilder directed William Holden as a cynical prisoner of war and an irresponsible playboy. Name the two films.

C. Which Wilder movie includes this line: "It's going to be you and me together, straight down the line."?

D. Jack Lemmon is a favorite Wilder actor. In which movie did he play an American tycoon who comes to Italy to reclaim the body of his father?

E. In which Wilder film did Audrey Hepburn play Maurice Chevalier's daughter?

V. Mervyn LeRoy

A. Which of the following classic Warners' musicals was directed by LeRoy: *42nd Street*, *Gold Diggers of 1933*, *Footlight Parade*?

B. In the forties, LeRoy directed a number of performances that received Academy Award nominations. Only one of these performances received the award. Was it Greer Garson for *Madame Curie*, Ronald Colman for *Random Harvest*, or Van Heflin for *Johnny Eager*?

C. LeRoy directed 1949 remakes of films originally directed by George Cukor and Ernst Lubitsch. Name these LeRoy films.

D. Which of the following film versions of successful stage plays was *not* directed by LeRoy: *Teahouse of the August Moon*, *No Time For Sergeants*, *A Majority of One*, or *Mary, Mary*?

E. Over the years, LeRoy directed Spencer Tracy in two films. One was *Thirty Seconds Over Tokyo*. Was the other *The Old Man and the Sea*, *The Devil At Four O'Clock*, or *The People Against O'Hara*?

(Answers on page 158)

114

Otto Preminger directing Richard Widmark on the set of
SAINT JOAN (1957)

MOVIE PEOPLE

Admittedly, this is not an easy quiz, since it deals with the people who work behind the cameras and usually shun Hollywood's "glamour" spotlight. But they contributed a great deal to films, and deserve to have a place in this book.

You are asked to match the person in the left column with the brief description of his or her particular talent or credentials, as cited in the right column.

Hermes Pan .... Director, noted for kaleidoscopic effects in
                            song-and-dance numbers
Yakima Canutt .... MGM's Art Director for many years
Max Fleischer .... Advisor on all Technicolor films, 1933-1963
Travis Banton .... Long-time screenwriter: *The Champ*,
                            Dinner at Eight, etc.
Harry Cohn .... Composer, won Academy Award for *High Noon*
Dorothy Arzner .... Producer of *Airport* and *Lost Horizon* (1973)
Marni Nixon .... Designer for *Gigi* and *My Fair Lady*
Dudley Nichols .... Dance director, associated with Fred Astaire
                            in the thirties
Stanley Donen .... Handled stunts for many films
James Wong Howe .... Costume designer for Mae West in the thirties
Cedric Gibbons .... Director of *Dracula* and *Freaks*
Dimitri Tiomkin .... Screenwriter, one of the "Hollywood Ten"
Frances Marion .... Producer associated with *King Kong*
                            (original version)
Busby Berkeley .... Powerful head of Columbia Pictures
                            for many years
Cecil Beaton .... Director of *On the Town*, *Funny Face*,
                            Lucky Lady, etc.
Julius J. Epstein .... Screenwriter: wrote *The Informer*, *Stagecoach*, etc.
Rouben Mamoulian .... Cinematographer: *Kings Row*, *The Rose Tattoo*, etc.
Edith Head .... Director of *Christopher Strong*, *Craig's Wife*
Dalton Trumbo .... Screenwriter: *Four Daughters*,
                            My Foolish Heart, etc.
Natalie Kalmus .... Author of the screen's Production Code in 1930
Merian C. Cooper .... Singer who has dubbed the voices of many stars
Erich Wolfgang Korngold ..... Director of 1932 version of *Dr. Jekyll and
                            Mr. Hyde*
Tod Browning .... Animator, created Popeye, Betty Boop
Dudley Nichols .... Award-winning designer: *The Heiress*,
                            Samson and Delilah, etc.
Will Hays .... Composer, won Academy Award for
                            The Adventures of Robin Hood

(Answers on page 158)

Judy Garland rehearses the minstrel show finale of BABES ON BROADWAY (1941). She is watched by director Busby Berkeley, seated on a stool in the foreground.

LUCIEN BALLARD

by Judith M. Kass

It is an axiom of filmmaking that the best cinematography is unobtrusive, almost invisible. Since it never calls attention to itself, Lucien Ballard's work generally goes unnoticed, but he has long been one of Hollywood's most gifted cameramen.

Ballard was born in Miami, Oklahoma in 1908. He was thrown out of several universities, journeyed to China, and worked for a while as a surveyor. In 1929, he was in Los Angeles where a friend was a script girl at Paramount. He visited her on the lot during night shooting, and before long, someone asked him to help out, loading cameras onto trucks and doing odd chores. Paramount asked him to work there officially but they paid $22.00 at most, so Ballard declined until the offer was raised to $35.00 for night work, which allowed him to keep his daytime job at a lumber yard.

Ballard was a helper, then an assistant cameraman, working first on a Clara Bow film. He was an assistant on Ernst Lubitsch's films with Jeanette MacDonald, then on *Morocco* (1930), working for Lee Garmes. At this point Joseph von Sternberg noticed him; Sternberg shot *The Devil Is a Woman* (1935) himself, with Ballard assisting him directly. An eye-filling icicle, this is Sternberg's coldest film and his last with Marlene Dietrich. Sternberg took Ballard to Columbia where he photographed *Crime and Punishment* (1935) and the last film for his mentor, *The King Steps Out* (1936). Where Sternberg's use of shadow is the dominant visual motif of *The Devil Is a Woman*, light, blinding and pure, is the salient feature of *The King Steps Out*, an otherwise undistinguished vehicle for Grace Moore and Franchot Tone. Softly lit and romantic, it is a typical, ornately decorated Sternberg film of the period.

Sternberg and Ballard had a disagreement; Sternberg left Columbia, but Ballard remained for the next three years. His first film on his own was a first-rate effort, *Craig's Wife* (1936), directed by Dorothy Arzner. Ballard's brilliantly overlit cinematography emphasizes the antiseptic environment Harriet Craig has made for herself. The baby spots Ballard bought especially for this film create an immaculate and sterile ambience for the cold and obsessive Mrs. Craig, played by Rosalind Russell.

Ballard wanted a raise and when it was refused, he immediately found work at RKO. One of his early projects there was shooting 16mm tests for *The Outlaw*, with Howard Hawks. They worked in Howard Hughes basement, and Ballard wanted to shoot a test with Jane Russell, who had been hanging around asking him questions. Ballard is responsible for the ingenious cross-

lighting which accentuates her physical attributes and implies a voluptuous sensuality the actress never realized in her subsequent roles. Once the film went on location in Flagstaff, Arizona, Hawks and Hughes began fighting with the result that both Hawks and Ballard were replaced, by Hughes himself as director and by Gregg Toland as cameraman. At Toland's request, Ballard remained on the picture, shooting the second unit. Filming was completed in 1940, but the movie was not released until 1943, and didn't go into general release until 1946.

From 1941 to 1946 Ballard worked at Fox. Only a few of his films during this period are of more than passing interest, although *Tonight We Raid Calais* (1943) is notable for the dark, brooding quality Ballard's lighting casts over the Nazi-occupied French town.

Ballard's most arresting photography during these years at Fox—he returned to the studio from 1951 to 1955—was for *Laura* (1944) and *The Lodger* (1944). When *Laura* was approximately 75 percent completed, director Rouben Mamoulian and Ballard were replaced by Otto Preminger and Joseph La Shelle, respectively. However, Ballard remembers working on *The Lodger* with pleasure: "I'd always wanted to do fog the way I did it in *The Lodger*. Before then it was always a grey haze. I did it with the fog in spots, with black and white definition still coming through." When the film's disgruntled producer told him that the fog didn't really look like that in London, Ballard replied, "... that's how it *should* look."

The Lodger makes no attempt to conceal Jack the Ripper's identity, so it relies heavily on the dazzling chiaroscuro effects Ballard and director John Brahm achieve by using the fog to create an atmosphere of suspense and tension. Ballard employs a hand-held camera to suggest the Ripper's terrifying advance on his prey. Mounted policemen tearing through the glistening streets are shot from either above or below, and at one point, a constable shines his light directly at the lens. Ballard's low-key lighting, with the Ripper's massive form suddenly looming up in the night, is a great asset in perpetrating *The Lodger*'s civilized horror.

Ballard met Merle Oberon while filming *The Lodger*. During the time they were married, from 1945 to 1949, they made five films together. The most interesting of these, *Berlin Express* (1948), was one of the first to exploit post-war Europe as a background. Ballard's cinematography is almost documentary in feeling, and, under Jacques Tourneur's direction, purposely undramatic. The shock of seeing Europe in rubble, particularly the

THE KING STEPS OUT (1936). With Franchot Tone and Grace Moore. Photographed by Lucien Ballard

THE KILLING (1956). With Elisha Cook, Jr. and Marie Windsor. Photographed by Lucien Ballard

WILL PENNY (1968). With Charlton Heston and Jon Francis. Photographed by Lucien Ballard

devastation of Berlin, is sufficient; no photographic virtuosity is required.

After *Laura*, Ballard, who was tired of having to answer to many people, decided to freelance. He also opted *not* to work in color because he felt that color consultants interfered with the cinematographer's control. When he finally did work in color, Ballard took on the added burden of dealing with 3-D. The film was *Inferno* (1953) and he managed to do it with as few tricks as possible. Ballard first worked in CinemaScope, a shape that few directors like and cinematographers customarily deride, in 1954. He is sanguine on the subject and merely notes that his preferred ratio is close to the old screen size, although he has no objection to Panavision.

In *Fixed Bayonets* (1951) Samuel Fuller and Ballard create a claustrophobic tension by avoiding the use of wide-angle lenses and confining their Korean War soldiers to cramped areas, such as the cave in the raw, snow-laden wilderness. Ballard's bleak photography complements Fuller's view of the world as an arena where death is a constant threat.

Ballard started filming Westerns late in his career, but was fortunate in being associated with two masters of the genre, directors Budd Boetticher and Sam Peckinpah, working first with Boetticher on *Buchanan Rides Alone* (1958). Ballard and Boetticher had collaborated earlier—on *The Magnificent Matador* (1955) and *The Killer Is Loose* (1956)—and Ballard had quickly become a favorite of Boetticher's. Thus, Ballard was able to make the transition to shooting Westerns as painlessly as he had gone from being a master of interior lighting to filming outdoors—on *Berlin Express*.

Boetticher's films are terse, shorter than the average feature, and packed with action. Ballard's camera circles easily within a compact group, stopping at times to notice some by-play or detail of character within a motionless frame. As he dollies with certain individuals, Ballard will slowly focus on a dark figure, signifying danger, off in the distance.

Interspersed with his memorable efforts for Boetticher from 1955 to 1960 are some minor but effective crime dramas—*Murder By Contract* (1958) and *Pay or Die* (1960). His best work in this genre was again with Boetticher—*The Rise and Fall of Legs Diamond* (1960)—and *The Killing* (1956) with Stanley Kubrick. On *Legs Diamond*, Ballard and Boetticher pre-exposed the film to make it look old and grainy so that the stock footage, with which it is intercut, is indistinguishable from the film Ballard shot. They also reproduced the uneven lighting from the twenties and thirties so that either Ray Danton (Legs) would virtually disappear from underlighting or Karen Steele (Alice) would look bleached out. Boetticher recalls his collaboration with Ballard: "I went to see Lucien Ballard, my favorite cameraman," and "we looked through all the twenties and thirties films. At that time they didn't have any of the modern techniques such as the

120

THE WILD BUNCH (1969). Photographed by Lucien Ballard

use of the crane. The only camera movement they knew was the pan. We decided to cut out all modern camera effects, such as dolly shots and traveling shots except those which are strictly functional. We also avoided putting people and things in the foreground to emphasize depth. We went back to the old flat lighting. It looked quite ugly at first sight." The producer went crazy when he saw the footage, but Jack Warner supported Boetticher so that he and Ballard were allowed to complete the picture as they liked.

The Killing (1956) is a black, deliberately ugly film of sordid surroundings, grubby, pathetic people, and failed dreams. Ballard, under Stanley Kubrick's direction, frequently frames the protagonists through bars, symbolic of either their present, limited existences, or of their futures. Elisha Cook, Jr. is a cashier at the race track

where the robbery Sterling Hayden has planned takes place. Cook is seen behind the grille of the betting window; in other scenes the supports of a spiral staircase and the rails of an iron bed enclose his face, placing him prematurely in the prison which is the logical end of this doomed enterprise. Shadows through windows also form bars. During the heist, Hayden stands against a wall on which the sun, struggling fitfully through the dirty glass, indicates the course of his future.

Ballard encloses the action in tight frames, relying on single source lighting to isolate the characters in their surroundings and to create a prison of shadows, a claustrophobic atmosphere, laden with suspicion. As Hayden outlines his scheme to his partners, Ballard shoots down onto a table where a pool of light illuminates the men's hands and faces, leaving a black, ominous ring

121

around them. Hearing a noise, they move cautiously into total darkness, symbolizing the danger they fear, and then into a dimly lit room to discover who's at the door. Faces are usually in half shadow, seldom fully exposed in bright light, as though to indicate the conspiracy of which these people are a part.

Ballard's other contributions include a series of fluid, repeated tracking shots which enable Kubrick to speed the action up and illustrate the precision of Hayden's plan. As Hayden enters a bus station to leave a package, a rifle concealed in a box of flowers, in a locker, Ballard tracks before him, stops at the locker, then tracks back to the door. When Joseph Sawyer picks the gun up, Ballard duplicates the shot from the same angle, enforcing the idea that the scheme is proceeding on schedule. Kubrick's other motive for the complex series of repeated actions, more than what is indicated here, is to interlock each character's movements, making each dependent on the others, and to give the feeling of inexorable progress toward a common fate.

Ballard's camera pans with Hayden as he restlessly paces the area between the bar and the betting windows, or remains motionless on Hayden and his girl (Coleen Gray), as in the course of their escape, Hayden tries to persuade the airline officials to let him carry his oversize bag, containing the money, onto the plane. The tension created by mercilessly focusing on Hayden's dilemma is almost unbearable.

Ballard's first film with Sam Peckinpah, *Ride the High Country* (1962), was one of the five seminal Westerns of the sixties; three of the remaining four—*The Wild Bunch, Will Penny* and *True Grit*—were also photographed by Ballard. By a not so curious coincidence, given America's national mood of disillusion, all five—the fifth is *El Dorado* (1967)—are concerned with aging, the passing of legend into history, the waning of a virtually mythological era in this country. Although all four are obviously distinct from each other, the thematic unity required that Ballard find a visual motif which would underscore, but not overpower, each film.

Both *Ride the High Country* and *True Grit* use autumnal landscapes as visual correlatives to growing old, with snow as a secondary note—the mining camp of the former, and the graveyard at the close of the latter. The clean purity of the light in the early sequences of *High Country*, the crisp, almost visible air, disguise the fact that the film is primarily concerned with sin, and with men's need to justify their misdeeds. Ballard shoots into the sky—he claims that MGM's water towers made any other angle impossible—but the effect is to ennoble Joel McCrea and Randolph Scott as they embark on their dubious mission, and to create an ambivalence in the audience's mind as to each man's real motives.

Ballard talks about working with Peckinpah: "Before shooting *The Wild Bunch* (1969) we pored over movies and stills having to do with the Mexican Revolution. We were both taken by the shallow, flat effect of these images. We selected our lenses in an attempt to recapture this same kind of visual texture. We wanted a yellow, dusty feeling, a washed out black-light-brown effect. We went down there and everything was green! I was making tests with filters for a week, and finally we got pretty much what we wanted."

In *The Wild Bunch* Ballard takes advantage of Texas and Mexico's naturally sandy terrain to ally the antiheroes with age and the imminence of death. Dust implies dessication; the members of the Wild Bunch are played-out, yet oddly optimistic men whose every step leads them closer to the death they at first avoid, then determinedly embrace.

Ballard's use of dust is subtle, never obvious, as in the opening when the bunch arrives in San Rafael, and rides through the tan, unpaved streets. The swirls of dust raised by the battle between the railroad gang and the bunch are matched by the powder from their gun blasts. The dominant color changes from tan to blue as the bunch leaves Texas to enter Mexico; Ballard emphasizes this as he matches the line formed by the bunch riding on the horizon with the line the railroad gang makes rushing forward in pursuit.

The merging of the two colors provides an elegaic tone for the villagers' farewell to the bunch. The first note of color, a red flower given to Warren Oates, supplies a note of optimism for an enterprise—the last job—which is surely doomed. The sun's rays striking through the trees heighten this false sense of hope. Later, at the baths, the rising steam is used to recall the dust, and to temporarily rejuvenate the spirits and the exhausted bodies of the bunch.

The most arresting shot takes place on a bridge the bunch blows up. A line of riders and horses, their hooves almost remaining parallel to the planking, falls into a river. The shot is taken in slow motion so that every

THE WILD BUNCH (1969). Photographed by Lucien Ballard

detail, elbows jerking upward, hair flying, coattails and hats jerking in the air, carefully records the ignominy of the surprised gang. The audience responds viscerally to the audacity of the shot, drawing in its breath as they fall, and laughing at the hapless gang, unexpectedly getting its first bath in months.

As the bunch walks doggedly to rescue Jaime Sanchez from Emilio Fernandez (the general) they take on a mythological dimension through Ballard's succession of abbreviated tracking shots. The ensuing battle is filmed in slow motion intercut with shots of the carnage taken at regular speed. This is an immense undertaking, a gut-wrenching conflagration of blood and bullets, a catharsis succeeded immediately by the final passage which is both elegaic and repulsively earthbound.

A line of buzzards corresponding to the lowering sky above waits for the gang to clear out, as Robert Ryan, his job done, slumps exhaustedly at the edge of the town. Ballard's camera rises on a crane to take in the desolate, sandy panorama as the bunch's lone survivor, Edmond O'Brien, asks Ryan to join him for whatever comes next. Their laughter, contemplating an uncertain future, is overlaid with shots of the bunch laughing at the irony of stealing a load of washers they took at the beginning.

The passage of the bunch into history is accomplished through a reprise of their departure from the village, a positive, gentle image with which to end a violent, negative film.

Two of Ballard's three remaining films with Peckinpah, *The Ballad of Cable Hogue* (1970) and *Junior Bonner* (1972) are also concerned with aging, the last frontiers and the absence of options. In *Cable Hogue* cinematographer and director again use dust and sand as symbols of age and death, and water, as in *The Wild Bunch*'s steam bath, as an emblem of rejuvenation.

The Getaway (1972), Ballard and Peckinpah's last film together, is substantively less interesting than their earlier movies. Although it received generally poor reviews, Pauline Kael, writing in *The New Yorker*, singled out Ballard's work for praise: "Lucien Ballard's near-abstract cinematography is so clean and muscular it deserves a subject . . ." On the film's set Ballard talked about working with Peckinpah to Grover Lewis (*Academy All the Way*): "Sam is the most talented director in Hollywood. Sam and I don't collaborate in any strict sense. We worked most closely together on *Ride the High Country* and *The Wild Bunch*. We spent months of preparation on each of those. I respect him and I enjoy working with him."

In 1968, Ballard photographed *Will Penny*, his first film with Tom Gries, a director whose unromantic view of the West complements Peckinpah's. *Will Penny*, too, is concerned with aging, for which Ballard again uses dust and snow. From the opening shots of cowboys waking on a cold morning to the final scene of carnage in the snow, Gries and Ballard visually create a world where one is seldom warm, and the fire that heats the body is unable to thaw the soul. *Will Penny* is a film of tans and browns, of dust and soil, and ultimately, of freezing snow, a symbol of Will's inability to grasp his last chance for love and a family.

In *True Grit* (1969), the earth and snow of the previous Westerns become warmer, more hopeful, giving way to an autumnal russet and gold and paralleling the growing bond between the aging marshal (John Wayne) and the girl (Kim Darby). The tranquil images Ballard achieves in two of his most spectacular shots—the deceptively peaceful hut in the river valley, and the leaf-covered clearing—are undercut by the ferocious action which succeeds these placid views: Dennis Hopper's hysterical chicken plucking and the shooting in the house, then Wayne's mad charge across the clearing toward the villains. Even at the end, when the talk turns to death in a snow-covered graveyard, director Henry Hathaway contradicts the idea of mortality by having Wayne, "the one-eyed fat man," leap the fence and gallop away.

Although Ballard has worked steadily since *True Grit*, few of the films he's photographed have reached the heights achieved by those he helped to make in the sixties. *Breakheart Pass* (1976), Ballard's most recent film, is a

TRUE GRIT (1969). With John Wayne, Glen Campbell, and Kim Darby. Photographed by Lucien Ballard

Charles Bronson railroad Western which reunites him with Tom Gries. This is a bleak-looking movie which begins with the soggy dark leaves and slush of a dismal train stop and ends in a wilderness of deep snow. The look of the film seems to complement Bronson's features, which become gloomier, almost hewn out of rock, as he ages. The one shot which demonstrates Ballard's cinematic virtuosity is the slow motion wreckage of a troop train wherein the camera picks out every broken splinter of the wooden cars as they hurtle into a gorge. The shots of Bronson climbing around the outside of the train might seem hard to attain, but over the years, the difficult has become routine, the unattainable ordinary. It's no surprise that at the age of 68, Lucien Ballard makes the impossible seem effortless.

Ballard knows that he isn't the main creative force behind a film: "A cameraman cannot do a picture the way he wants to, because he's not the boss. It's a collaboration of the director, the art director, and the cameraman. I'd sacrifice photography anytime for the sake of the story."

In interviews Ballard is candid; he's aware of his own abilities and values them highly. He says, "I feel that I can save [producers] money being in a picture from the beginning."

Ballard praises his working relationship with Peckinpah: "Sam uses me both as his eyes and as a sounding board. I can come up with specific suggestions and I know that he will listen to me and seriously consider them." He continues in the same vein, "I want to contribute to a picture, not just work on it. I'm their man if they want more than a cameraman."

SALUT, BIENVENUE, DROP DEAD:
The French Director in Hollywood

By Stephen Harvey

Hollywood has often been rebuked for preventing innovative artists from trespassing beyond its hermetically sealed studio gates. According to conventional wisdom, movie moguls choose to worship at the altar of the glass-windowed box office rather than in the temple of Thespis and Art. And, undoubtedly, American-born filmmakers of an idiosyncratic bent have generally been made about as welcome in Hollywood as peasants at a Czarist reception.

Yet for those who have made their artistic reputations elsewhere, the response has always been much more inviting. For more than half a century, Hollywood's inferiority complex concerning the supposedly advanced culture and sophistication of Europeans has allowed innumerable foreign directors the dubious chance to forsake UFA, Pathe and Svensk Filmindustri for a sojourn in the alien compounds at Burbank and Culver City.

The first great wave of gifted Europeans arrived here in the twenties, for reasons that had more to do with cold-blooded economics than with the refined cinematic taste of the likes of Adolph Zukor and William Fox. Already on the verge of dominating the world movie market, Hollywood had begun to feel the competition of its more enterprising European rivals. By offering Europe's foremost talents more money than their home studios could afford, Hollywood instantly transformed its former rivals into its own salaried employees. As Europe's most vital production center, the German film industry became the prime target, and such legendary directors as Murnau, Lubitsch, E. A. Dupont and Paul Leni succumbed to Hollywood's terms, as did Scandinavians Mauritz Stiller, Victor Seastrom and Benjamin Christensen, Hungarians Paul Fejos and Alexander Korda, and innumerable others throughout Europe. The impact of these directors on the American silent film was profound and immediate.

Yet, while such movies as Lubitsch's *Forbidden Paradise*, Seastrom's *The Wind* and *The Scarlet Letter*, Leni's *The Cat and the Canary*, Stiller's *Hotel Imperial* and Murnau's *Sunrise* were among the highlights of the silent era, these directors encountered a dilemma that was to become all too familiar to their successors. For all the prestige these movies engendered, the mass American audience tended to find them a trifle esoteric. Moreover, used to relative autonomy abroad, Stiller, Murnau *et al* were ill-equipped to cope with the regime of intrusive production heads and their notions of machine-like speed and efficiency ruling unchallenged. Hence, in the name of order, economy and boffo b.o., these filmmakers found themselves penalized for exactly those distinctive qualities which had attracted the Hollywood bosses to their European work in the first place.

The arrival of sound brought the fatal blow to many European careers in Hollywood. European-born directors were at an obvious disadvantage to their American counterparts in the nuances of coaching actors in idiomatic English, while the early talkies' static visual approach crippled the flair for stylization which had been these directors' hallmark. By 1932 death and emigration home had so decimated the ranks that among the major European figures only Lubitsch remained.

Political developments overseas prompted the next foreign inundation; during the late thirties it became clear that while Nazism was the worst fate to ever befall the Old World, indirectly it had a most salutary effect on Hollywood. Actors, writers, producers and artisans of all description arrived in search of asylum and work; by the time of the U.S. entry into the war, the likes of Billy Wilder, Douglas Sirk, Fritz Lang, Robert Siodmak and Otto Preminger were firmly ensconced in Hollywood. Many of them proved out of necessity to be much more flexible than their Teutonic predecessors of the twenties; it's rather ironic that such wholeheartedly American movies as *Fury, The Major and the Minor, Double Indem-*

Charles Laughton in TALES OF MANHATTAN (1942). Directed by Julien Duvivier

A scene from FLESH AND FANTASY (1943), directed by Julien Duvivier. The central figures: Edward G. Robinson and Thomas Mitchell

nity and *Laura* should have been directed by the likes of Lang, Wilder and Preminger.

Oddly enough, while the studio guards at Paramount, Fox and the rest were nearly trampled by the incoming stampede of German-speaking moviemakers in the prewar years, the French remained coolly aloof to Hollywood's blandishments. Before 1935, among important Gallic directors only Jacques Feyder succumbed to an American contract, tarrying long enough to direct Garbo in *The Kiss* and the German-language version of *Anna Christie* plus a few inconsequential Garbo-less efforts before making a speedy departure. Perhaps the French resisted Hollywood because they were trained in a rather fragmented school of movie-making which encouraged low-budget experimentation, while Lang and the rest were more readily prepared to cope psychologically with the glossy American movie factories, which after all resembled UFA on a slightly larger scale.

However, the fall of France rendered such qualms irrelevant. A few of the major filmmaking talents, such as Marcel Carné, opted to remain in France and work under the tacit gaze of the Nazis. Many others, however, found this prospect impossible even to contemplate. Jacques Feyder emigrated to neutral Switzerland for the duration, while Julien Duvivier, René Clair and Jean Renoir, who enriched the French cinema of the thirties, opted to take their chances in Hollywood.

Upon their arrival in the U.S., they were to receive a decidedly mixed welcome. Thanks to their exalted reputations abroad, and with many of their American counterparts working for the government for the duration, these three had no trouble securing lucrative con-

tracts with the major studios. The catch was that Hollywood was by no means prepared to acquiesce to the quaint European notion that the job of directing was anything more than one major cog in the immense production machine. For their part, these Gallic emigrés balked at the rigid studio hierarchies, to them as exotic and incomprehensible as Hindu castes in India, and snorted disdainfully at the blandly impersonal polish applied as a matter of course to the production line American product. Considering this impasse, it's remarkable that these three directors managed to get anything accomplished at all during their sojourn in Hollywood. Yet between them they managed to direct thirteen features in Hollywood, none of which was without interest.

Of the three, Duvivier should have been the most easily adaptable to the new scheme of things. The director of such renowned pre-war films as *Poil de Carotte, David Golder* and *Pepe Le Moko*, Duvivier used an approach which could perhaps have been best likened to that of William Wyler—literate, technically expert, sensitively acted, yet emanating a slightly impersonal chill. For all his sophistication and proficiency, Duvivier was no iconoclast à la Clair or Renoir; his work rarely engendered the tumultuous controversy often greeting their films both in France and abroad during the thirties. Moreover, unlike his two compatriots, Duvivier had some idea of what he was in for in Hollywood. Before the war, Duvivier had spent one frustrating year at MGM, mostly involved with directing *The Great Waltz* (1938). When MGM summarily assigned a series of other directors, including Josef von Sternberg, to supply the finishing touches to this opulent film, Duvivier angrily departed for France, gutturally muttering his intention never to submit to such an indignity again.

These years later a chagrined and presumably wiser Duvivier found himself once more in Hollywood. In the United States, his most lauded film had probably been *Un Carnet du Bal*, an episodic tale of a dowager's sentimental journey to find the beaus whose names had filled her dance card in her youth. Hence it's hardly coincidental that three of Duvivier's four American films bear more than a passing resemblance to his earlier triumph. This was particularly true of *Lydia* (1941), Duvivier's first American project, which so resembles *Carnet* that it practically constituted self-plagiarism. Based on a story coauthored by Duvivier and produced by Alexander Korda as a vehicle for his then-wife Merle Oberon, *Lydia* relates the belated reunion of an elderly Boston spinster with her suitors of yore, during which she explains via flashback why she never chose to marry any of them. Mounted with great elegance, this tale singularly failed to eclipse the memory of *Carnet* for contemporary critics or bemuse much of the paying audience, thanks to Duvivier's languid pacing and Oberon's somewhat one-dimensional performance in a role which called for an all-out tour-de-force.

After *Lydia*, Duvivier went to Twentieth Century-Fox for *Tales of Manhattan* (1942). This must have seemed highly promising in the planning; the studio's first all-star dramatic extravaganza, it consisted of a string of O. Henryish vignettes linked by the symbol of a man's dress jacket descending the social scale from the haute monde of Charles Boyer and Rita Hayworth past New York sophisticates Henry Fonda and Ginger Rogers, struggling conductor Charles Laughton and ex-bourgeois Bowery derelict Edward G. Robinson, before coming to rest in the black shantytown principally inhabited by Paul Robeson and Ethel Waters. Upon the film's release, this last episode stirred up considerable ire for its simple-minded racial stereotypes; Robeson himself was so incensed that he vowed never again to act in another film. The rest of the film proved certainly less offensive but scarcely more distinguished. On the whole, Duvivier was apparently too overwhelmed by a flaccid scenario and the thick veneer of Fox's production gloss to infuse any life into most of his cast. Paradoxically, the most intriguing thing about *Tales of Manhattan* lies moldering unseen somewhere in the depths of Fox's vaults. Duvivier had filmed a sixth sequence featuring W.C. Fields and said evening jacket, but it was excised for reasons of length before *Tales* was released, and hasn't turned up since.

Undaunted, Duvivier once more toyed with the anthology form in Universal's *Flesh and Fantasy* in 1943. Although conceived on a somewhat more intimate scale than its predecessor, *Flesh and Fantasy* featured an unusually prepossessing cast for a studio like the Universal of the forties; as co-producer as well as director, Duvivier mustered a roster that included Barbara Stanwyck, Betty Field, Robert Cummings and *Tales* alumni Edward G. Robinson and Charles Boyer, who also served as Duvivier's co-producer. Linked by a common theme of fate and predestination, the three stories are a bit glib and ponderously ironic, but at least Duvivier managed to endow *Flesh and Fantasy* with the kind of vivid imagery which *Tales of Manhattan* so thoroughly lacked.

The first vignette, concerning a cynical crone (Field) turned dewy beauty during Mardi Gras, provides the excuse for a profusion of chiaroscuro expressionistic effects. Likewise the Robinson episode of a level-headed attorney turned murder-obsessed fanatic contains a nightmarish, paranoid intensity which anticipates Fritz Lang's masterful *Woman in the Window*, filmed with the same star the following year. With the exception of Robinson, however, the performances have a somnambulistic air not entirely justified by the mystical kitsch of the three scenarios to which they were assigned. *Flesh and Fantasy* was, relatively speaking, Duvivier's best regarded work in America at the time, but the critics were really responding to the novelty of its pretensions rather than any genuine artistic achievement.

With *The Impostor* (1944), his final American film,

Duvivier finally managed to elude the spectre of *Un Carnet du Bal* for the first time since his arrival in Hollywood. Reunited with Jean Gabin, the star of *Pepe Le Moko*, Duvivier shifted to contemporary melodrama to suit the gruff sensitivity of this actor in his second and last American film. This story of an ex-con who joins the Free French Army in Africa under an assumed identity ought to have been ideal for these two war-exiled expatriates, but it's mainly just reminiscent of such other contemporary efforts as the Bogart/Curtiz *Passage to Marseille*, and Gabin gave an oddly colorless and uncharismatic performance. After *The Impostor*'s indifferent reception, both he and Duvivier returned to France at the war's end with no apparent regrets.

On his return Duvivier resumed his position as the grand old pro of the French film industry, becoming once more as prolific as he had been in the thirties. Duvivier's failure to make any real impression in Hollywood can't really be blamed on the meddlesome stance of the studios which so afflicted Clair and Renoir; as his own producer in two cases, Duvivier enjoyed as much working freedom as his most respected American counterparts. Rather, Duvivier's melange of irony and melancholy romanticism seemed stilted and anemic wrenched out of his native idiom, a problem magnified by his seeming inability to direct actors persuasively in a language that remained resolutely alien to him.

The language barrier seems to have posed no such dilemma for René Clair, whose four American features possess a fluency and vitality which Duvivier's efforts here lacked. Like Duvivier, only more successfully, Clair had worked in English before the war, having helmed the

Fredric March and Veronica Lake in I MARRIED A WITCH (1942). Directed by René Clair

AND THEN THERE WERE NONE (1945). With (left to right) C. Aubrey Smith, Louis Hayward, Queenie Leonard, Richard Haydn, Walter Huston, and Roland Young. Directed by René Clair

disarming fantasy *The Ghost Goes West* and the less remarkable *Break the News* in Britain. The difficulty was that Clair, a sober-minded theoretician who made effervescent satires, naively assumed that if the powers-that-were hadn't appreciated his independent turn of mind, they wouldn't have beckoned him to join their ranks in the first place.

Clair must have been somewhat mystified to discover that his first American assignment was to concoct a vehicle for Marlene Dietrich, then in residence as Universal's femme fatale. Exotic demi-mondes were hardly in Clair's usual line, but matters could have been worse—one blanches to think what he would have made of Deanna Durbin, Universal's other principal box-office attraction at the time. What Clair came up with was *The Flame of New Orleans* (1941), the saga of a female rake's progress through nineteenth-century Creole society. This film was in many respects an odd throwback to Dietrich's baroque outings with Josef von Sternberg; once more she is cast as a glamorous adventuress, photographed through numberless layers of gauze as she picks through the spoils of her well-heeled conquests before sacrificing her all for the sake of one virile, integrity-ridden male. Clair's contribution was to provide the requisite transplanted-Gallic ambience and to endow the film with a touch of lighthearted ribaldry in place of Sternberg's murky eroticism.

Clair's next two works once more found him purveying the sort of whimsy and good-humored satire of *Le Million* and *The Ghost Goes West*, albeit in somewhat diluted form. In fact *I Married A Witch* (1942), the story of a ghost of an incinerated Salem witch (Veronica Lake)

who haunts a stuffy New England politician (Fredric March) seems to have been a deliberate attempt to recapture the appeal of *Ghost*, and to a certain degree it succeeded. Based on a story by Thorne Smith, the creator of the Topper stories, *I Married A Witch* rather lacks the visual élan of Clair's best French work, but its heroine's seductive guile and bitchy prankishness is diverting enough. Most applauded at the time was Lake's blithe impersonation of the witch; before Clair had divined her sense of humor (and, unfortunately, usually thereafter), Lake had been merely a blank-faced siren peering stonily from behind that famed cascade of hair. In the long run, *I Married A Witch* probably meant more to her career than it did to Clair's.

After contributing a short sequence to *Forever and a Day* (1943), a wartime all-star cavalcade praising the valor of our British allies, Clair turned to *It Happened Tomorrow* (1944), probably the most imaginative and personal of his American efforts. Scripted by Clair and Dudley Nichols, the film's central premise is both witty and foreboding—a turn-of-the-century cub reporter (Dick Powell) mysteriously gets a peek at future news headlines the day before, giving him a scoop on every constable and reporter in town, as well as the fright of his life when he reads of his own demise hours before it is due to take place. Laced with the slapstick mayhem and frantic chases of such earlier triumphs as *The Italian Straw Hat* and *A Nous La Liberté*, *It Happened Tomorrow* is also reminiscent in the best sense of Preston Sturges' farces of the same period.

Clair's last American film is paradoxically both the best regarded of the lot in many circles, yet one which Clair himself has since repudiated. *And Then There Were None* (1945), the first of three screen versions of Agatha Christie's *Ten Little Indians*, is probably the most expert and stylistically faithful movie adaptation of Christie to date, *Murder on the Orient Express* notwithstanding. Witty, smoothly paced, and consummately well crafted, it features a genuinely surprising dénouement and particularly adroit ensemble work from a top-heavy coven of character actors, including Walter Huston, Barry Fitzgerald, Roland Young, and Judith Anderson. Yet Clair's retrospective disdain is quite understandable; *And Then There Were None* is a clear case of a director's vision made totally subservient to the material he was hired to translate to the screen. Twentieth Century-Fox desired the use of Clair's obvious technical proficiency and nothing more; Clair delivered what was required but his heart obviously wasn't in it. Decrying the bland, faceless expertise that he viewed as the Hollywood ideal, Clair returned home after the war to make *Le Silence Est D'or, La Beauté Du Diable* and others for which he could once more feel a strong personal commitment.

Of the three directors considered here, Jean Renoir was and remains the most profound artist, and his American career was by far the most paradoxical. Having endured endless clashes with film financiers in France, unlike Clair and Duvivier he would gladly have remained here to work after the war if the studios had been amenable; yet the critical and financial failure of *Diary of a Chambermaid* sadly rendered that impossible. Seemingly the most inveterately French of all directors, in Hollywood Renoir preferred to try his hand at quintessentially American subject matter, feeling that France could never be accurately evoked within the confines of an American sound stage. As usual Renoir's instincts proved justified; *Swamp Water* and *The Southerner*, his two essays in Americana, are insightful and moving works filled with an affection for his land of exile, while the ostensibly French-localed *This Land is Mine* and *Diary of a Chambermaid* emanate an airless, sterile quality.

On first glance, *Swamp Water* would seem to have been more suited to the likes of John Ford, who, in fact, made the similar *Tobacco Road* at the same studio, also in 1941. Yet this story of a young Georgia boy's attempt to clear the name of a swamp hermit accused of murder is endowed with Renoir's own distinctive brand of humanism and commitment. Renoir filmed *Swamp Water* in part on location in the Okefenokee swamps—a rare phenomenon in itself in those days—and beyond its great visual beauty, like *The Southerner* this film conveys a rare sense of the indissoluble bond that links country people and the land they inhabit.

Though *Swamp Water* proved a moderate success financially, its box-office returns were insufficient to heal the rift between Renoir and production head Darryl Zanuck. Zanuck demanded studio retakes of some of the location footage and at one point threatened to take Renoir off the picture and replace him with someone more acquiescent. The result was that Renoir never again toiled for the studio he dubbed "Fifteenth Century-Fox."

After a series of aborted projects, Renoir proceeded to RKO for *This Land Is Mind* (1943), which he co-wrote with the omnipresent Dudley Nichols as well as directed. An unabashed exercise in wartime propaganda, *This Land Is Mine* tells of the transformation of a timid, mother-dominated schoolteacher into a heroic martyr to the Nazis, intended to symbolize the valor of all Occupied France. The fact that its sentiments were unarguably in the right place compensated for a lot in 1943, and the film provides a likely showcase for one of Charles Laughton's standard bravura turns in the main role, but *This Land Is Mine* nonetheless remains Renoir's least interesting American film. For one thing, unlike almost all of Renoir's work it completely lacks a secure sense of milieu; in a self-conscious stab at universality, the decors resemble an architectural back-lot no man's land left over from Chaplin's *The Great Dictator*. Moreover, as usually occurred when Dudley Nichols strove to instruct the masses with profound human statements (*The Informer, Mourning Becomes Electra*, etc.), the film is peopled with a gallery of bloodless abstractions spouting ponderous generalities which signify very little in any genuine sense.

With *The Southerner*, two years later, Renoir created a work as profound and evocative as *This Land Is Mine* was empty and pretentious. As with many of his great films, the key is his surface simplicity. The spare narrative of a year in the life of a sharecropping family attempting to start their own farm in the face of uncooperative neighbors, illness and the harsh Texas climate, *The Southerner* expressed more of the beauty of human endurance than did all the self-conscious rhetoric of Renoir's collaboration with Dudley Nichols. Like *Swamp Water, The Southerner* was largely filmed far from the confines of a Hollywood sound stage, with California's dusty San Joaquin Valley standing in convincingly for Texas. American audiences and critics unfamiliar with *Toni*, Renoir's earlier rural masterwork, were particularly taken with *The Southerner*'s air of understated naturalism.

The subsequent *Diary of a Chambermaid* (1946) proved far more controversial. Once more sealed inside a never-never-land sound-stage France, Renoir selected Mirbeau's acrid novel of an ambitious servant-girl and the havoc she wreaks on a decadent upper-class household as the basis for a wry dissection of the rigid class system of an earlier age, with implications for our own. *Diary* has a bitter, detached flavor missing in his earlier American work, and the France it depicts is far removed from the rather benign vision presented in *This Land Is Mine*. Yet it too is marred by Renoir's inability to conjure a genuinely Gallic atmosphere out of an English-language script performed by American actors toiling in a studio in California. Although the film's claustrophobic hothouse quality is probably not quite what Renoir in-

Anne Baxter and Dana Andrews in SWAMP WATER (1941). Directed by Jean Renoir

129

Zachary Scott and Betty Field in THE SOUTHERNER (1945). Directed by Jean Renoir

tended, the film is enlivened by the off-beat characterizations of Francis Lederer, Burgess Meredith (Renoir's co-producer and co-scenarist), and Judith Anderson. Paulette Goddard's work as the flirtatious heroine represented an admirable attempt to add a greater dimension to the superficial soubrettes she usually portrayed.

Most importantly, *Diary of a Chambermaid* was a clear harbinger of the Renoir who was to emerge in the next decade; while thematically it harkened back to the peerless pre-war *The Rules of the Game*, stylistically it anticipated the deliberate heightened artifice of his autumnal masterworks, *The Golden Coach* and *French Can-Can*. Lacking this perspective, contemporary audiences could hardly have been blamed for finding *Diary of a Chamber-maid* a singularly baffling enterprise.

Bafflement would be too mild to describe the reception accorded *The Woman on the Beach*, Renoir's final American project, upon its release in 1947. Even after drastic re-editing reduced it to a scanty seventy-odd minutes, critics and the small audience it attracted pronounced it turgid and interminable. Far more idiosyncratic even than *Diary of a Chambermaid*, this film resembles nothing so much as an oddly slanted rehash of Fritz Lang's film noir treatises on sexual obsession, even featuring Lang's favorite tramp-heroine Joan Bennett as its star. Certainly Lang's usual tone of doom-laden misanthropy would have been ideally suited to this tangled triangle between a violent, blind ex-painter (Charles Bickford), his restless spouse (Bennett) and an angst-ridden war veteran (Robert Ryan). As these figures plot and counterplot against each other, in Renoir's less deterministic hands their motivations seem to shift with every reel change, underscored by a profusion of forties pop-Freudian fire-and-water images and the raging crescendoes of Hanns Eisler's intrusive score. The whole film seems to take place in some nightmarish subterranean trance where the usual notions of logic and coherence have no place.

The Woman on the Beach garnered neither money nor prestige for the powers at RKO, and Renoir's six-year Hollywood sojourn came to an inauspicious close. As Renoir has acknowledged in his memoirs, what it ultimately came down to was Darryl Zanuck's perception that "Renoir has a lot of talent, but he's not one of us." Zanuck's appraisal couldn't have been more accurate, but the loss was Hollywood's. In later years an invigorated Renoir pursued his career in France, Italy and even India; ironically, in retirement he has chosen to spend his days in Beverly Hills, having outlived the regime which both nurtured and thwarted his work in those long-gone years of exile.

THE MOVIE SONGSMITHS (TWO)

As in the first *Movie Buff's Book*, we are asking you to match the movie songsmith with his song and with the film in which the song appeared:

"Easy to Love"	Irving Berlin	*She Loves Me Not*
"By Strauss"	Nacio Herb Brown	*Flying Down to Rio*
"My One and Only Highland Fling"	Harold Arlen	*Gigi*
"Now It Can Be Told"	George Gershwin	*Born to Dance*
"Never Gonna Dance"	Frederick Loewe	*State Fair*
"It's a New World"	Jule Styne	*The Barkleys of Broadway*
"All I Owe Ioway"	Vincent Youmans	*Swing Time*
"Small World"	Jerome Kern	*Three Little Words*
"Sunday, Monday, or Always"	Harry Warren	*Alexander's Ragtime Band*
"You Are My Lucky Star"	Ralph Rainger	*An American in Paris*
"Love In Bloom"	Bert Kalmar	*Dixie*
"They're Either Too Young or Too Old"	Cole Porter	*Gypsy*
"Orchids in the Moonlight"	Richard Rodgers	*A Star Is Born*
"The Night They Invented Champagne"	Jimmy Van Heusen	*Thank Your Lucky Stars*
"Thinking Of You"	Arthur Schwartz	*Broadway Melody of 1936*

(Answers on page 159)

THREE LITTLE WORDS (1950). With Fred Astaire and Vera-Ellen

HITCH

By Patrick McGilligan

Hitch, as he likes to be called, always dresses in a navy blue or black suit, decorated by the thin, red Legion of Honor ribbon. His assistants also dress severely, in respect, a strange formality in the Hollywood of today. The set evokes an Old World, not merely closed (as it is) but hermetically sealed, a throwback or capsule of time. Hitch dominates it by sheer presence, and by a reputation that visibly awes his crew. They eye him distantly, turn quiet when he approaches, call him "sir." Short, plump, old, his is the most famous profile in film. He bobs when he walks, like a sea-tossed buoy, and his bowling ball figure is, like his movies, at once scary and comic.

On a June day, between takes, a chauffeur waits to drive Alfred Hitchcock back to his bungalow, also on the Universal City lot. He will await the next call there. Or, if things are moving swiftly, he will sit inside his mobile van, just sit there, clasping fat, pink hands thoughtfully, his face impassive. The small room has a writing desk, pencils, a full-length mirror, three leather chairs and a rolled copy of The Sunday Times and Telegraph. It is here, in this silence, that Alfred Hitchcock will endure the ordeal of filmmaking, which can last so very, very long in its delays.

His assistant director, young and harried, in suit and tie, appears to present a line-up of children for a Sunday School sequence the following day. Hitchcock himself looms in the doorway, solemnly and wordlessly inspecting the scrub-brushed kids whose mothers wait expectantly nearby. A few murmured words to his assistant, and two lucky girls and a boy are chosen. The director returns to his lair. His assistants are legion, devoted, constantly astir. They make many of the minor decisions during shooting, while the director sits like a grim, inscrutable buddha, the secret ruler of all he surveys.

Three or four women, especially, long-time personal assistants, supervise the progress of the production. Once the key subordinate was secretary Joan Harrison, rumored to be the minister of casting; she went on to become the trusted producer of television's "Alfred Hitchcock Presents." Today, as ever, the central figure is "Madame" (Mrs. Hitchcock) Alma Reville, once a script girl, and editor and assistant director in England, later a co-scenarist on many Hitchcock features. He is utterly attached to her. Her exact contribution is a mystery, but she appears on the set with regularity, whisking Hitch away to privacy.

The master of suspense is 75, encumbered with a pacemaker and shooting his 53rd movie, one half-century after he began his celebrated directorial career with *The Pleasure Garden* in Munich, Germany. Last, with George

Cukor, of the active early-sound veterans, Hitchcock has rarely varied his personal film style since 1952. The new movie, which he wrote in collaboration with Ernest Lehman over a two-year span, is called *Family Plot*, based on a novel by Victor Canning that involves two plots, a kidnapping and a fake psychic. It will be familiar Hitchcock terrain: innocent persons drawn into a web of sex, fear and crime. It stars Karen Black, Bruce Dern, William Devane and Barbara Harris—although the real star, of course, is Hitch.

* * * *

Born on Aug. 13, 1899, in London, Alfred Hitchcock, as a lad, studied mechanics, navigation and art, among other things, before signing on to pen titles for Paramount's Famous Players-Lasky in England at age twenty-three. He shortly became immersed in all aspects of film production (credited, for example, with the adaptation, dialogue, assistant direction and art direction for *Woman to Woman* in 1922), and ultimately a director. In his native England, he directed such classics as *Murder* (1930), *The Man Who Knew Too Much* (1935), *The 39 Steps* (1935) and *The Lady Vanishes* (1938), before moving to Hollywood, under contract to David O. Selznick, in 1939. In America, Hitchcock flourished, creating such masterworks as *Rebecca* (1940), *Suspicion* (1941), *Shadow of a Doubt* (1943), *Notorious* (1946), *Strangers on a Train* (1951), *Rear Window* (1954), a second version of *The Man Who Knew Too Much* (1956), *Vertigo* (1958), *North by Northwest* (1959), *Psycho* (1960), *The Birds* (1963) and *Frenzy* (1969)—to name a certain few.

Perhaps no other film director has achieved his international stature (François Truffaut once compared him to Kafka, Dostoyevsky and Poe) and, what's more, his common-day box-office popularity. Even the average moviegoer is versed in the Hitchcockian credo: the essential but trivial plot gimmick or what Hitchcock calls the "MacGuffin" (the uranium samples in *Notorious*); the stress on pure, visual cinema and montage (over 70 shots in 45 seconds in the *Psycho* shower scene); and his expected cameo appearance in nearly every Hitchcock picture (in a newspaper's weight-loss advertisement in *Lifeboat*). The signatorial walk-on was "strictly utilitarian" at the beginning, Hitchcock has said, later a superstition and gag, and finally a "rather troublesome gag" that distracted the audience. Still, the cameo is part of Hitchcock's carefully cultivated public image, and he takes it seriously. He banned all visitors and non-essential crew from the set on the day he shot his own appearance in *Family Plot*—fittingly, as a shadow behind the door of

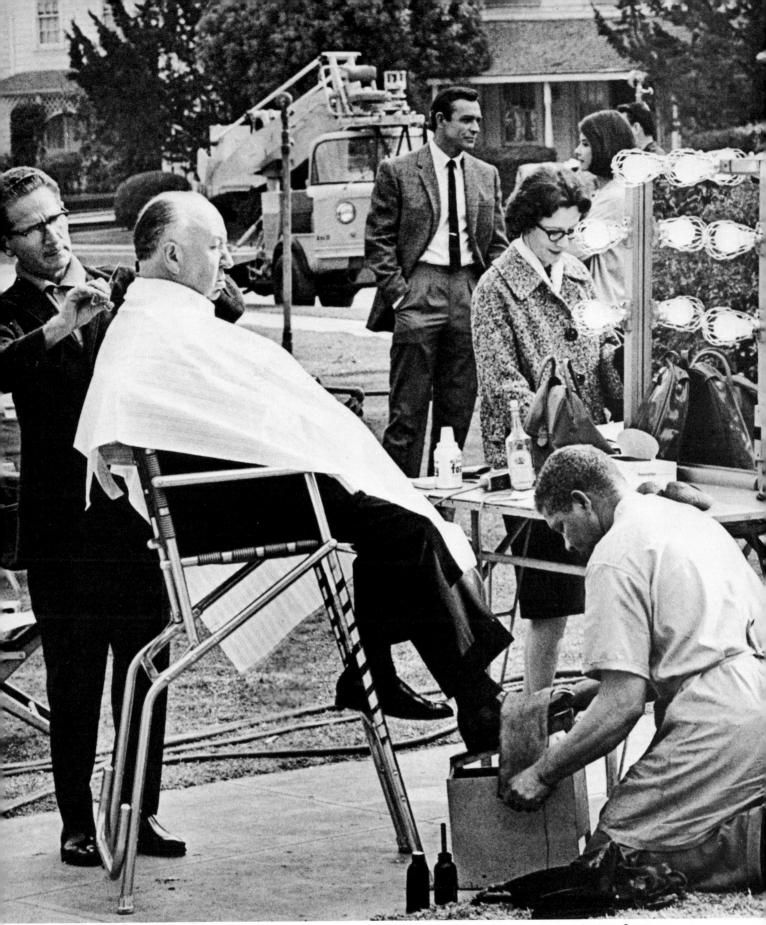

Alfred Hitchcock gets a haircut on the outdoor set of MARNIE (1964). In the background: stars Sean Connery and Diane Baker

Alfred Hitchcock's FAMILY PLOT (1976). With William Devane and Karen Black

the Registrar of Births and Deaths.

The June heat was oppressive, even inside the drafty Universal sound stages, as *Family Plot* was being shot that summer. The unit publicist was besieged by buffs and scribes, everybody convinced that Hitchcock was directing his last picture. The director himself only chuckled at this thought, and then pointed to his Universal contract (he is actually believed to own a small percentage of the studio), which calls for two more. Yet, he often seemed subdued, languid, almost bored. I found him, one afternoon, resting in his mobile van, and I asked him whether moviemaking was still as much fun as it once was—fifty years ago.

"There are so many imponderables today," he said, in his sticky, macabre drawl. He raised an eyebrow. "Costs are so much higher, and therefore the watching of costs becomes half the operation. One time, when costs were low, we didn't care. We just shot and shot. In the days of the silent pictures, we always shot out of continuity because we didn't have the quality of character in those days. But now people say to me, 'Well, can you do this particular scene, because, cost-wise, it makes it easy for us to do the picture.' I say, 'Yes, but wait a minute, you're choosing a scene at the end of the picture, and I don't know my character until I've shot the first scene.'

"I'm giving you an example of how the economics are liable to sometimes interfere with the flow of the character and narrative which you have in your mind, and that is one of the problems you have to face today. It takes a lot of the fun out of it because there isn't that freedom that you like to have, ideally. The way one would like to shoot a film would be in its continuity of narrative.

134

"I will say this," he continued, "In my personal experiences, I am not pressed at all. They ask my personal production unit, 'Is it possible to do this?' I have to say, 'Well, it can be done, but it's going to be difficult.' In a sense, freedom of activity, which I have, becomes an embarrassment, because I have a duty not to spend money all over the place. Although they like to talk about film art, there is an element of industry in it.

"We know that film is an art form of the twentieth century, but it carries with it many liabilities. What would a painter think if I handed him a canvas and said that it cost $750,000; here's an easel which costs $500,000; here's a box of paints which costs $250,000; here's a pallette which costs $800,000; and a set of brushes that costs $500,000. Now paint me a picture, and at least get me my money back. The artist would say, 'You're crazy.' "

Hitchcock directs from his chair, seated, virtually immobile, but for an occasional tilt of the head, a nod, a grunt of approval or the rare, humorous quip. He studies each scene with apparent disinterest, puffing his Dunhill cigar leisurely, and giving directions, when necessary, in a dry, ponderous voice. Mainly, he converses with his director of photography (Leonard J. South, who operated the camera for the late Robert Burks on many Hitchcock films), his assistant director, and the script girl. Scenes are normally accomplished in one or two takes. I asked him whether he is ever surprised by what ends up on the screen.

"No-o-o," he replies, a slight smile playing on his lips, as he elongated the word. "I know the film by heart, cut by cut. Don't forget, I've been an art director, I've been a scriptwriter, I've been an assistant director. I've done all the jobs in this business. A lot of directors haven't. They've come from writing or the theater. Not to say that they aren't good but they are, to some extent, in the hands of the technicians.

"As you noticed, you've never seen me look through the camera. The reason is because there is a rectangular screen. That's what we're aiming at and, in my mind, I can see a screen. I can talk to the cameraman in his own language. 'Where are you cutting, give her a haircut, do this, do that.' So all the technical side is very second nature to me."

* * * *

Of the acting side, the stories about Hitch are rife. It is said that he once compared all actors to cattle; he himself cannot remember ever having precisely said such a thing, although he has been questioned about it ever since his arrival from England. More likely, he says with a patented leer, he said all actors *behave* like cattle. Acting is the least important element of his cinema; because he is, in some ways, a disciple of Pudovkin's theories, his actors are frequently called upon to emote less rather than more. Only Hitchcock knows that they may end up as little more than an eyeball in a particular scene. He talks little with them, as a rule. Casting is the last step, rendered almost as an afterthought.

Through the years, there have been notorious battles. And, indeed, a close reading of *Hitchcock*, François Truffaut's conversations with the master, reveals that Hitch was never really satisfied with anybody, save the reliables Cary Grant and James Stewart. To Ingrid Bergman, during the making of *Under Capricorn* (1949), he offered this consolation, "Ingrid, it's only a movie!"; he clashed repeatedly with Kim Novak during the shooting of *Vertigo* (1958). Often repeated is his advice to Paul Newman, when the "method" star approached him during *Torn Curtain* (1966) to inquire about his motivation. "Learn your lines," Hitchcock supposedly informed him, "And don't speak to me until after the film." It seems that this unsavory reputation has been with him as early as 1941, when he directed his only screwball comedy, *Mr. and Mrs. Smith*. Carole Lombard ribbed him one day by building a three-sectioned corral on the set, with a young cow in each, name-tagged for the three principals, Lombard, Robert Montgomery and Gene Raymond.

There were minor skirmishes, too, during the making of *Family Plot*. Roy Thinnes, originally cast in the movie, was replaced shortly after shooting began on the vague complaint from Hitchcock that he was not "strong enough" (which may mean that he was, in fact, too strong). Hollywood wags point out that Hitchcock at his press conference in the local cemetery earlier in the month, kept referring to Thinnes as Roy Scheider. The director said it was a slip of the tongue, but more whimsical observers saw malice aforethought. The movie, after all, was being called *Deceit* in those early days.

Karen Black, no small star nowadays, and a free-spirited devotee of scientology, brushed mildly with Hitchcock over her role, a kidnapper who, in one scene, must disguise herself as an oldish woman. She is required to play the part (over her protestations) with an unnaturally husky voice, lowered on Hitchcock's command to heighten her malevolence. Her efforts to inject some personality into the dialogue were met with typically Hitchcockian reminders to stay low-key. One day, Black made an amusing mistake that tested their goodwill. Generously, she informed Hitch about the "loose thread" on his otherwise immaculate suit, only to realize instantly, by his droll sangfroid, that she was indicating his beloved Legion of Honor ribbon. They nevertheless managed to strike up a friendly rapport; her good humor won out. One day, as shooting droned on endlessly and tensions rose, she fondled the back of Hitchcock's head, as he sat mute and wary. If shooting was delayed much longer, she purred, she would gladly telephone his dog. The director surrendered with a deep, rolling laugh.

But worrying most, almost complaining, during my visit to the *Family Plot* set, was the man who replaced Roy Thinnes, an actor named William Devane who was impressive on television as JFK in the much-praised re-enactment of the Cuban Missile Crisis. Devane, a talented actor who in the spring of 1975, also directed an acclaimed Los Angeles production of Eric Bentley's *Are You Now Or Have You Ever Been*, met Hitchcock only five minutes before his first scene. Devane was to play the key villain. The director told him, "You're William Powell," and later, only "Be lighter, lighter."

"I can add three colors to his pallette if he'll let me know what's going on," Devane explained. He was talking during a break in his dressing room, alternately grimacing and chuckling over the situation. "He's not interested in what makes the people tick. He's interested in what makes the story tick. I've seen this character in every film Hitchcock has ever made.

"One day, I had a line, saying 'You know how funny well-to-do people are.' He asked me, 'Would it be too much trouble to say rich?' I said to him, 'Only a lower-class person would say rich. Someone born to money would say well-to-do.' He thought a minute and then said exactly the same thing back to me. I said, 'Wait a minute. That's exactly what I said to you.' He said, 'Go ahead and fake it.' He doesn't talk at length about anything. He ends up by saying, 'Fake it.' "

The conversation whetted Devane's appetite for a confrontation, and he walked smoothly over to Hitchcock's mobile lair, and entered determinedly. Moments passed. Not a raised voice could be heard. Finally, Devane emerged, with the same lost, head-shaking expression. "He didn't reveal anything to me," he explained. "He just continued to explain to me how the film was being shot. I said, 'You'll let me know if we're going in opposite directions?' He said, 'Yes.' "

Alfred Hitchcock's FAMILY PLOT (1976). With Bruce Dern and Barbara Harris

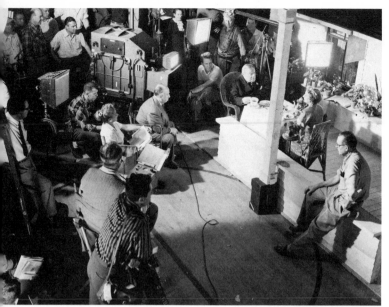

Hitchcock directing on the set of THE TROUBLE WITH HARRY (1955). At tea: Edmund Gwenn and Mildred Natwick

Devane laughed resignedly.

"It's tiring to work with a genius."

But Hitch usually has his favorites, in this case Bruce Dern and Barbara Harris, who play the psychic medium and her boyfriend-cabbie. They are the more interesting roles, to his way of thinking, and he lavishes attention on the actors who play them. Dern (once affectionately called a "calf" by Hitchcock) could practically coax laughter at will from the veteran director, whom he so admired that he visited the sets on off-days to quietly observe his technique. Dern worked with Hitchcock once before, when, as a sailor, he was fatally bludgeoned in "Marnie." He even managed to discuss character with the director one day for half an hour, although, admittedly, it was a one-sided talk.

"I did all the talking," Dern explained, "He opened up by saying, 'Bruce, it's been a long time.' I said, 'Yeah, twelve years. The last time you saw me, you had me beaten to death with a fire poker.' He said, 'Yes, who would ever have thought you would end up being my leading man, much less a leading man at all?' I said, 'If you hang in there long enough, it can happen to anybody; if it can happen to Jack Nicholson, it can happen to me.' Then we talked a little bit about the wardrobe; he told me to lighten my hair; and I suggested a few things to him about the character.

"He doesn't get in the actor's way at all. I don't know what everybody's been talking about all these years. Once you're in his form—there's no changing that, at all, for anyone—then you have the freedom to do what you want. He doesn't give you things to do, but when he does give you something to do, you do it, because he's absolutely right. You can't fight him, you must accept the fact that he is the best. Once you do that, you're in."

With Barbara Harris, Hitchcock seemed positively polite and gracious, a consideration that shows in her merry performance. Directing a critical psychic seance, he even went so far as to stand and gesture balletically to demonstrate an especially difficult movement in her trance. He thanked her for her perspicacity after the lengthy scene, and when she wondered aloud whether that complicated word had anything to do with sweat, he remarked with dry wit: "Perspicacity has nothing to do with the underarms; it means alertness." Everyone broke into laughter.

"I know what I want, but you don't always get it," he remarked later of his performers, still entrenched in his mobile van. "Some of them are extremely efficient. They can take direction very easily. 'Slow down, speed up, make this point.' " He grinned like a pumpkin. "I have an actor in this picture—Bruce Dern—well, he's absolutely surefire. One sees an actor like Bruce, and you see a tempo. You say, 'Speed it up there, and don't make that pause so long.'

"They're very different," he continued, "from the method actor who says, 'I don't know what I might do there; I have to feel it.' They're not very helpful in this business. They may be fine in the theater. But they're taught to improvise which, to me, is a very risky word. They're taught that at schools! I remember an actor saying, 'Well, I went to such and such a school, and I was told to improvise.' I said to him, 'That's not improvising; that's writing.'

"And what for? What for?"

The silence was thunderous. He asked the question as if it answered itself, spreading his palms slightly; for a director who so meticulously plans everything, in his head and on paper, before arriving on the set, it was the utmost heresy. "I improvised in the office a year ago on this," he said, thrusting his fleshy, lower lip forward into a pout, "I don't have to improvise." I left him there alone, as I found him, staring noiselessly into space, as the set whirled in preparedness outside. No doubt he was thinking up something gruesome—for actors and audiences alike—for Hitch's 54th.

THE MASTER OF MENACE

Elsewhere in this book, you'll find an article on Alfred Hitchcock's approach to his films. Here's a quiz devoted entirely to his films—a tribute to the masterly director who has delighted, surprised, and frightened moviegoers for so many years.

1. In which Hitchcock films will you find the following characters: a) Rupert Cadell b) John "Scottie" Ferguson, and c) Ben McKenna. And who played these roles?

2. Which film is evoked by each of the following: a) a name written on the window of a train b) a murder reflected in the glasses of the victim, and c) a windmill turning against the wind?

3. In which Hitchcock movie does a) Sylvia Sidney kill Oscar Homolka b) Barry Foster strangle Anna Massey, and c) Grace Kelly stab Anthony Dawson?

4. A Hitchcock fan should be able to answer the following questions and, of course, provide the titles of the films to which they refer:

a) What are Uncle Charlie and his niece doing on the platform of a moving train?

b) What's inside the chest displayed so prominently in Profesor's Cadell's apartment?

c) Why did the sea gull gash Melanie Daniels' forehead?

5. Which of the following actors has never appeared in a Hitchcock movie: Ray Milland, James Mason, Raymond

Bonus Photo Question:
Alfred Hitchcock directed only one romantic comedy. Here's a scene from this 1940 movie, with Carole Lombard and Gene Raymond. Its name?

Massey, Sean Connery?

6. In which movie is there a long and harrowing murder sequence involving, among other things, a kettle of boiling soup, a carving knife, and a gas oven?

7. As you no doubt know, Hitchcock makes a brief appearance in every one of his films. In which movie was he seen as a party guest sipping champagne?

8. It's all relative: who played a) Jane Wyman's father in *Stage Fright* b) Cary Grant's mother in *North By Northwest*, and c) Teresa Wright's mother in *Shadow of a Doubt*?

9. With the exception of Ingrid Bergman, Cary Grant's leading ladies in his Hitchcock movies have been cool and elegant blondes. Name the cool and elegant blonde who played opposite Grant in each of the following roles (and, of course, name the film): a) Lina MacKinlaw b) Frances Stevens, and c) Eve Kendall.

10. Exactly what is *The Trouble With Harry*?

11. Twice, Farley Granger has entered into unholy pacts that result in murder, once in *Rope* and then in *Strangers on a Train*. Name the actors who played his partners-in-crime in each of these movies.

12. This 1969 Hitchcock movie sweeps from a Virginia mansion to a Harlem hotel to a Cuban hacienda. Its name?

13. *The Wrong Man*, Hitchcock's 1957 release, starred Henry Fonda as a) a man wrongly accused of spying for the Russians b) a man wrongly identified as a homicidal killer, or c) a man wrongly accused of theft?

14. Name the actress who made her film debut in each of these Hitchcock movies: a) *Jamaica Inn* b) *The Trouble With Harry*, and c) *The Birds*.

15. Everyone remembers the horrifying shower murder of Janet Leigh in *Psycho*. But who played Anthony Perkins' *other* on-camera victim in the film?

16. Who played the leading role in Hitchcock's original 1934 version of *The Man Who Knew Too Much*? Was it a) Clive Brook b) Roger Livesy, or c) Leslie Banks?

17. Time for the oldsters: a) In which film did Ethel Barrymore play the unhinged wife of lecherous Judge Charles Laughton? b) In which film did Ethel Griffies play a tweedy ornithologist? c) In which film did Leopoldine Konstantin play Claude Rains' sinister mother?

18. Name the Hitchcock movie in which a key character is named Mr. Memory.

19. Hitchcock talking: "The heroine is Cinderella, and Mrs. Danvers is one of the ugly sisters." Which movie is he talking about?

20. Which Hitchcock movie contains characters named Sam and Henrietta Flusky?

(Answers on page 159)

LIGHTS! CAMERA! ACTION!

The set of virtually every movie is a beehive of activity, mixing talent and temperament in varying proportions. The mood may range anywhere from sober diligence to rampant hysteria.

Here, from the recent and the distant past, is a portfolio of photographs taken during the production of films you may—or may not—remember.

Richard Boleslavsky (left, with a pencil in his ear) directs Greta Garbo and Soo Yung in a scene from the 1934 film, THE PAINTED VEIL.

Garbo again, this time with Basil Rathbone, filming a wintry scene from ANNA KARENINA (1935). Seated behind the camera: Director Clarence Brown.

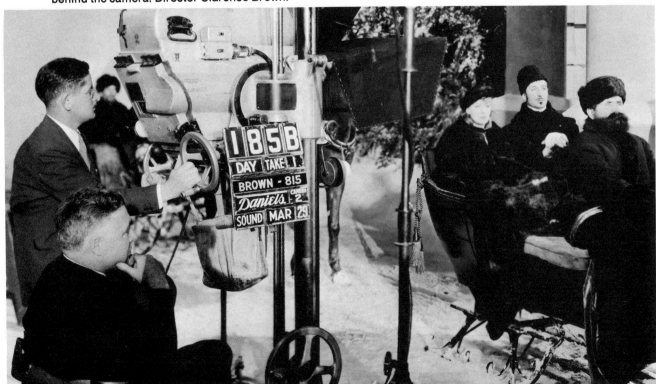

On the set of MARIE ANTOINETTE (1938), with director W. S. Van Dyke II and Norma Shearer

The year: 1932. Relaxing in front of Marie Dressler's dressing room are (left to right) Claire Du Brey, Norman Foster, director Sam Wood, Polly Moran, John Walters, and Miss Dressler. The movie: PROSPERITY.

Actor-director Lowell Sherman was originally assigned to direct BECKY SHARP in 1935. Here he is on the set with Miriam Hopkins and Frances Dee. During production Sherman died and was replaced by Rouben Mamoulian.

On the set of STAGE DOOR (1937), Katharine Hepburn examines the designs for her gowns with director Gregory La Cava.

Thirty years after STAGE DOOR, Katharine Hepburn discusses a scene for GUESS WHO'S COMING TO DINNER (1967) with co-stars Spencer Tracy, Katharine Houghton, and Sidney Poitier and director Stanley Kramer.

Director W. S. Van Dyke II instructs Jeanette MacDonald in her music hall number for the spectacular drama, SAN FRANCISCO (1936).

A striking production photograph on the set of BABES ON BROADWAY (1941). Atop the crane (in white) is director Busby Berkeley, giving instructions to Mickey Rooney, Judy Garland, and the chorus. (Somewhere among the bystanders is producer Arthur Freed.)

Jeanette MacDonald, getting the finishing touches on her coiffure. The movie: the Rodgers and Hart musical, I MARRIED AN ANGEL (1942).

Cameraman Ernie Bachrach photographs Dolores Del Rio and Gene Raymond for FLYING DOWN TO RIO (1933). At this moment, neither cameraman nor stars suspect that the real attraction of this movie will be two dancers named Ginger Rogers and Fred Astaire.

Director Jack Conway talks with stars Robert Montgomery and Nora Gregor as they prepare to film an idyllic scene for BUT THE FLESH IS WEAK (1932).

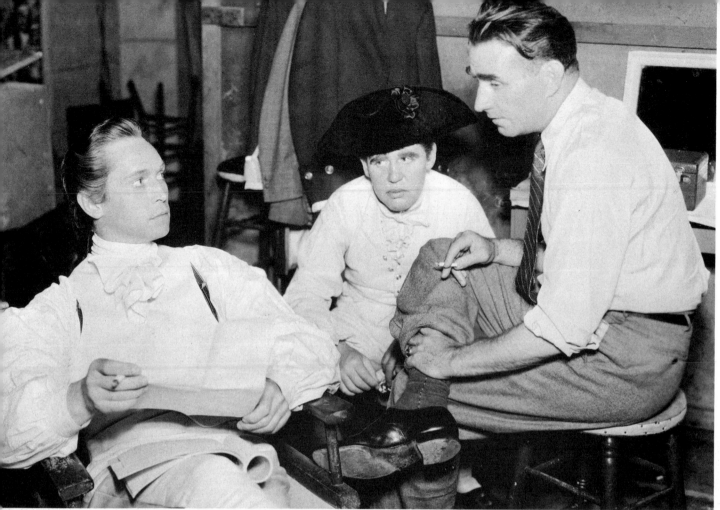

Franchot Tone, Charles Laughton, and director Frank Lloyd relaxing on the set of MUTINY ON THE BOUNTY (1935), in which Laughton played his famous role of Captain Bligh.

Director John Ford walks into a scene in TOBACCO ROAD (1941) to talk to his weary actors, Ward Bond and Gene Tierney. At right: Charles Grapewin as Jeeter Lester.

Director Lothar Mendes gives last-minute instructions to Charles Laughton and Verree Teasdale before shooting a scene for PAYMENT DEFERRED (1932).

James Mason and Deborah Kerr rehearse a scene for JULIUS CAESAR (1953), under Joseph L. Mankiewicz' direction.

The principal players, producer, and director of the epic film, QUO VADIS (1951) pose for a picture. In the front row, at Robert Taylor's left, is director Mervyn LeRoy. Seated next to him is producer Sam Zimbalist.

On location for SUDDENLY, LAST SUMMER (1959) with Elizabeth Taylor

A cheerful moment during the filming of TWO FOR THE SEESAW (1962), with stars Shirley MacLaine and Robert Mitchum and director Robert Wise

ANSWERS TO PUZZLES

EXTRY! EXTRY!

(page 21)

1. *Easy Living* (1937)
2. *Ace in the Hole* (also called *The Big Carnival*) (1951)
3. *The Miracle of Morgan's Creek* (1943)
4. *Made For Each Other* (1939)
5. *What Ever Happened to Baby Jane?* (1962)
6. *Across the Pacific* (1942)
7. *Rebecca* (1940)
8. *North By Northwest* (1959)
9. *Boy Meets Girl* (1938)
10. *Frenzy* (1972)
11. *It Should Happen to You* (1954)
12. *Gentleman's Agreement* (1947)
13. *The Last Hurrah* (1958)
14. *Key Largo* (1948)
15. *The Russians Are Coming, The Russians Are Coming* (1966)
16. *Cat People* (1942)
17. *The Philadelphia Story* (1940) or *High Society* (1956)
18. *Trial* (1955)
19. *20th Century* (1934)
20. *I Want to Live!* (1958)
Bonus Photo Question: *Marked Woman* (1937)

AREN'T WE ANGELS/DEVILS?

(page 22)

1. a) *The Bishop's Wife* (1947) b) *It's a Wonderful Life* (1946) c) *For Heaven's Sake* (1950)
2. Don Ameche played the rakish gentleman, Laird Cregar "His Excellency."
3. *Here Comes Mr. Jordan* (1941) and *Down to Earth* (1947)
4. c) Lionel Barrymore
5. a) *Damn Yankees* (1958) b) *All That Money Can Buy* (1941) c) *Rosemary's Baby* (1968)
6. Mason: *Forever, Darling* (1956). Astaire: *Yolanda and the Thief* (1945)
7. a) *Half Angel* (1951) b) *Angel* (1937) c) *We're No Angels* (1955)
8. b) *Heaven Only Knows*
9. a) *Alias Nick Beal* (1949) b) *The Greatest Story Ever Told* (1965) c) *Damn Yankees* (1958)
10. a) Paul Douglas
11. Nelson Eddy, Jeanette MacDonald
12. a) *The Devil and Miss Jones* (1941) b) *Hell in the Pacific* (1968) c) *The Devil Doll* (1936) d) *The Devil is a Woman* (1935) e) *Dante's Inferno* (1935)
13. *Between Two Worlds*
14. a) Diane Cilento
15. Rains was heavenly Mr. Jordan in *Here Comes Mr. Jordan* (1941) and devilish Nick in *Angel on My Shoulder* (1946)
16. *The Next Voice You Hear* (1950)
17. a) *Bedazzled* (1967) b) *All That Money Can Buy*, 1941) c) *Doctor Faustus* (1968)
18. a) *Eye of the Devil* (or *13*) (1967) b) *The Seventh Victim* (1943) c) *The Possession of Joel Delaney* (1972)
19. a) *Cabin in the Sky* (1943) b) *The Angel Levine* (1970) c) *I Married An Angel* (1942)
20. *The Horn Blows At Midnight* (1945)

CHUCKLES AND GUFFAWS

(page 24)

1. *The More the Merrier* (1943)
2. *The Major and the Minor* (1942)
3. *The Apartment* (1960)
4. *The Women* (1939)
5. *The Bride Came C.O.D.* (1941)
6. *It's a Gift* (1934)
7. *20th Century* (1934)
8. *All About Eve* (1950)
9. *You Can't Take It With You* (1938)
10. *The Thrill Of It All* (1963)
11. *Woman of the Year* (1942)
12. *Adam's Rib* (1949)
13. *The Awful Truth* (1937)
14. *Love Crazy* (1941)
15. *A Shot in the Dark* (1964)
16. *Ruggles of Red Gap* (1935)
17. *What's Up, Doc?* (1972)
18. *The Russians Are Coming, The Russians Are Coming* (1966)
19. *Ninotchka* (1939)
20. *Some Like It Hot* (1959)
21. *It Happened One Night* (1934)
22. *Holiday* (1938)
23. *The Lady Eve* (1941)
24. *Bringing Up Baby* (1938)
25. *Divorce, American Style* (1964)

LINES TO REMEMBER

(page 25)

1. *High Sierra* (1941). Ida Lupino
2. *Duel in the Sun* (1946). Gregory Peck
3. *A Day at the Races* (1937). Groucho Marx
4. *Shanghai Express* (1932). Marlene Dietrich
5. *Dracula* (1931). Bela Lugosi
6. *Meet Me in St. Louis* (1944). Margaret O'Brien
7. *Citizen Kane* (1941). Dorothy Comingore
8. *The Strawberry Blonde* (1941). James Cagney.
9. *Grand Hotel* (1932). Lewis Stone
10. *To Each His Own* (1946). John Lund
11. *Gaslight* (1944). Ingrid Bergman
12. *Wuthering Heights* (1939). Laurence Olivier
13. *Singin' in the Rain* (1952). Jean Hagen
14. *Mr. Skeffington* (1944). Claude Rains
15. *The Pride of the Yankees* (1942). Gary Cooper
16. *They Died With Their Boots On* (1941). Errol Flynn
17. *The Philadelphia Story* (1940). Katharine Hepburn
18. *My Man Godfrey* (1936). Mischa Auer
19. *The Little Foxes* (1941). Charles Dingle
20. *Hud* (1963). Paul Newman
21. *Mr. Deeds Goes to Town* (1936). H.B. Warner
22. *Goodbye, Mr. Chips* (1939). Robert Donat
23. *Top Hat* (1935). Fred Astaire
24. *Elmer Gantry* (1960). Arthur Kennedy
25. *She Done Him Wrong* (1933). Mae West

BLESS THE BEASTS

(page 34)

1. *Mighty Joe Young* (1949)
2. *Track of the Cat* (1954)
3. *Bringing Up Baby* (1938)
4. *Doctor Dolittle* (1967)
5. *Bell, Book and Candle* (1958)
6. *Them!* (1954)
7. *Smoky* (1946)
8. *State Fair* (1962)
9. *The Emperor Waltz* (1948)
10. *Mogambo* (1953)
11. *The Return of October* (1949)
12. *That Darn Cat* (1965)
13. *The Fox* (1969)
14. *National Velvet* (1944)
15. *The Fly* (1958)
16. *Hatari!* (1962)
17. *You Never Can Tell* (1951)
18. *The Blue Bird* (1940)
19. *Clarence, the Cross-Eyed Lion* (1965)
20. *Ring of Bright Water* (1969)

Bonus Photo Question: Cheetah

STAGE TO SCREEN

(page 35)

1. Shirley Booth.
2. d) *Merrily We Roll Along*
3. Rita Hayworth appeared in *Pal Joey* (1957), Mitzi Gaynor in *South Pacific* (1958), Gloria Grahame in *Oklahoma!* (1955), and Rita Moreno in *The King and I* (1956).
4. William Shakespeare. John Barrymore starred in *Romeo and Juliet* (1936); Joe E. Brown was featured in *A Midsummer Night's Dream* (1935); Elisabeth Bergner was in *As You Like It* (1936), and Elizabeth Taylor starred in *The Taming of the Shrew* (1967).
5. Raymond Massey. And Josephine Hull repeated her stage role in the movie.
6. c) *Mr. Music*
7. Walter Huston. On stage in *Knickerbocker Holiday* (1938). On screen in *All That Money Can Buy* (1941).
8. Lillian Hellman. Bette Davis starred in film versions of Ms. Hellman's *The Little Foxes* and *Watch on the Rhine*. Dean Martin appeared in the adaptation of *Toys in the Attic*. Shirley MacLaine was in the second film version of *The Children's Hour*. And Sylvia Sidney starred in the adaptation of *The Searching Wind*.
9. *They Knew What They Wanted*. *Ah, Wilderness!* became *Summer Holiday*; *My Sister Eileen* was musicalized under that title; *The Women* was remade as *The Opposite Sex*.
10. a) *A Majority of One* (1961) b) *Gypsy* (1962) c) *Craig's Wife* (1936), and d) *Oh, Dad, Poor Dad, Mama's Hung You in the Closet and I'm Feelin' So Sad* (1967)
11. *The Male Animal*
12. *Lady in the Dark*
13. Joey Evans, in *Pal Joey*. Gene Kelly played him on stage in 1940, Frank Sinatra on screen in 1958.
14. Katharine Cornell. Elizabeth Barrett Browning in *The Barretts of Wimpole Street*.

15. False—in one respect. In the 1953 version, the hero was played by Gordon MacRae, not Howard Keel.
16. Katina Paxinou
17. *Design For Living*, a play in early 1933, a movie later that same year.
18. b) *A Man For All Seasons*, in 1966
19. All played matchmaker Dolly Levi—Ruth Gordon in Thornton Wilder's play, *The Matchmaker*, Shirley Booth in the 1958 film version of *The Matchmaker*, Carol Channing in the original production of *Hello, Dolly!*, a musical adaptation of *The Matchmaker*, and Barbra Streisand in the 1969 movie version of *Hello, Dolly!*.
20. True. *The World of Henry Orient* was called *Henry, Sweet Henry*; *The Quiet Man* became *Donnybrook!*; *Pride and Prejudice* was musicalized as *First Impressions*, and *All About Eve* was turned into *Applause!*.
21. b) Jack Lemmon
22. Gertrude Lawrence. Joan Crawford played the Lawrence stage role in *Susan and God* (1940). Ginger Rogers took her role in *Lady in the Dark* (1944), and Deborah Kerr played her part in *The King and I* (1956).
23. a) *Guys and Dolls* b) *Cactus Flower* c) *Angel Street* (*Gaslight* on screen), and d) *Dream Girl*
24. Allan Jones, Joe Penner, Martha Raye, Rosemary Lane, Irene Hervey, Eric Blore.
25. Lee Tracy and Edmund Lowe

Bonus Photo Question: *The Member of the Wedding*. Brandon de Wilde, Julie Harris, and Ethel Waters.

MOVIES OF THE SIXTIES

(page 37)

1. Ralph Bellamy in *Sunrise at Campobello* (1960). Franchot Tone in *Advise and Consent* (1962). Fredric March in *Seven Days in May* (1964). Henry Fonda in *Fail-Safe* (1964). Peter Sellers in *Dr. Strangelove* (1964). Lee Tracy in *The Best Man* (1964) (as an ex-President).
2. a) All starred Rod Steiger. b) Stanley Kramer produced and directed all three films. 3) Lee Remick starred in all three movies.
3. Minnie Castevet: *Rosemary's Baby* (1968), Ruth Gordon. Dianna Scott: *Darling* (1965), Julie Christie. Sylvia Barrett: *Up the Down Staircase* (1967), Sandy Dennis
4. Ginger Rogers played Harlow's mother with Carol Lynley, and Angela Lansbury played the role with Carroll Baker.
5. b) "Call Me Irresponsible," 1963's Oscar-winning song by Sammy Cahn and James Van Heusen
6. a) Olivia de Havilland in *Lady in a Cage* (1964) b) Tallulah Bankhead in *Die! Die! My Darling!* (1965) c) Bette Davis in *Hush, Hush, Sweet Charlotte* (1965)
7. *Tunes of Glory*
8. *The Hustler*
9. a) Sue Lyon b) Jean Seberg c) Jane Fonda d) Nobody. This was merely a punning reference to the British novelist. e) Natalie Wood.
10. *The Graduate* (1967)
11. a) *The Birds* (1963) b) *The Hustler* (1961) c) *The Collector* (1965)
12. a) *Gypsy* (1962) b) *Finian's Rainbow* (1968) c) *Mary Poppins* (1964) d) *The Sound of Music* (1965) e) *Funny Girl* (1968)
13. Bette Davis
14. a) *A Guide for the Married Man* (1967) b) *Boys' Night Out* (1962) c) *Kiss Me, Stupid* (1964)

15. a) John Wayne. Lee Marvin b) Lee Marvin c) Charlton Heston d) Debbie Reynolds e) Paul Newman
16. Norman Bates: *Psycho* (1960), Anthony Perkins. Raymond Shaw: *The Manchurian Candidate* (1962), Laurence Harvey. Buck Barrow: *Bonnie and Clyde* (1967), Gene Hackman.
17. *One, Two, Three.* Arlene Francis
18. 1963: Sidney Poitier. 1965: Lee Marvin. 1967: Rod Steiger.
19. a) *A Walk on the Wild Side* (1962) b) *Elmer Gantry* (1960) c) *Thoroughly Modern Millie* (1967)
20. *How to Steal a Million*: Audrey Hepburn and Peter O'Toole. *How to Murder Your Wife*: Jack Lemmon
Bonus Photo Question: *Birdman of Alcatraz*

THE SPIRIT OF ADVENTURE
(page 45)

1. Melville Cooper, Basil Rathbone, Claude Rains
2. *The Thief of Bagdad* (1940)
3. Joan Fontaine
4. *King Solomon's Mines*
5. Gary Cooper
6. Sir Percy Blakeney: *The Scarlet Pimpernel.* Diego: Zorro as in *The Mark of Zorro*
7. c) *Storm Over the Nile*
8. *Under Two Flags* (1936)
9. *Northwest Passage* (1940)
10. Dana Andrews
11. Clark Gable
12. Richard Barthelmess
13. *The Sea Hawk* (1940)
14. Trevor Howard, Vanessa Redgrave, David Hemmings, John Gielgud, Jill Bennett
15. Douglas Fairbanks, Jr. in 1937; James Mason in 1952
16. *Beau Geste*
17. *The Three Musketeers.* D'Artagnan
18. b) Trevor Howard
19. *The Dawn Patrol*, made by Warners in 1930 and 1938
20. b) Burt Lancaster
Bonus Photo Question: *Unconquered.* Boris Karloff

RIGHT ON, LADIES!
(page 47)

1. Susan Hayward in *Top Secret Affair* (1957)
2. June Allyson in *The Girl in White* (1952)
3. Ingrid Bergman in *Spellbound* (1945)
4. Joan Crawford in *The Best of Everything* (1959)
5. Bette Davis in *June Bride* (1948)
6. Angela Lansbury in *State of the Union* (1948)
7. Rosalind Russell in *A Woman of Distinction* (1950)
8. Barbara Stanwyck in *Executive Suite* (1954)
9. Loretta Young in *Key to the City* (1950)
10. Ginger Rogers in *Lady in the Dark* (1944)
11. Natalie Wood in *Sex and the Single Girl* (1964)
12. Irene Dunne in *Together Again* (1944)
13. Katharine Hepburn in *Adam's Rib* (1949)
14. Jean Arthur in *A Foreign Affair* (1948)
15. Greer Garson in *Strange Lady in Town* (1955)
Bonus Photo Question: *Over 21*

"AND THE WINNER IS . . . "
(page 49)

1. John Garfield
2. c)*Mutiny on the Bounty*
3. *Come and Get It* (1936). *Kentucky* (1938). *The Westerner* (1940).
4. d)*My Fair Lady* (1964)
5. Best Director—Mike Nichols
6. c)"Que Sera, Sera"
7. Luise Rainer for *The Great Ziegfeld* (1936) and *The Good Earth* (1937). Katharine Hepburn for *Guess Who's Coming to Dinner* (1967) and *The Lion in Winter* (1968), shared with Barbra Streisand for *Funny Girl*
8. *The Discreet Charm of the Bourgeoisie*
9. b)Emil Jannings for *The Way of All Flesh* and *The Last Command*
10. b)Darryl F. Zanuck
11. c)*Guess Who's Coming to Dinner*
12. Clark Gable did not win as Best Actor. That honor went to Robert Donat for his performance in *Goodbye, Mr. Chips*.
13. Jeanne Eagels
14. c)Best Original Screenplay, to Herman J. Mankiewicz and Orson Welles
15. *The Last Angry Man*
16. b)*Sands of Iwo Jima*, in 1949
17. Eva Marie Saint and Barbra Streisand. Jennifer Jones had appeared in Westerns as Phyllis Isley. Audrey Hepburn was in British films in minor roles. Sandy Dennis had appeared in *Splendor in the Grass* in 1961.
18. Liv Ullmann.
19. a)*The Sin of Madelon Claudet*
20. Gene Hackman in *The French Connection.* Jane Fonda in *Klute.*
Bonus Photo Question: Both Burt Lancaster and Deborah Kerr were nominated but lost—Lancaster to William Holden for *Stalag 17* and Kerr to Andrey Hepburn for *Roman Holiday.*

THE SPORTING LIFE
(page 50)

1. a) Baseball. b) Tennis. c) Football
2. Clark Gable: *To Please a Lady* (1950). Paul Newman: *Winning* (1969). Steve McQueen: *Le Mans* (1971).
3. a) *Kentucky* (1938) b) *Maryland* (1940) c) *National Velvet* (1944)
4. Cornel Wilde. Tyrone Power was a bullfighter in *Blood and Sand* (1940), Robert Evans in *The Sun Also Rises* (1957), and Robert Stack in *The Bullfighter and the Lady* (1951).
5. *Pat and Mike* (1952). Katharine Hepburn played Pat, and Babe Zaharias played herself.
6. Milland discovered his serum in *It Happens Every Spring* (1949). MacMurray discovered his substance (flubber) in *The Absent-Minded Professor* (1961).
7. Robinson trained the Giants in *The Big Leaguer* (1953). Douglas managed the Pirates in *Angels in the Outfield* (1951).
8. c) *Indianapolis Speedway*
9. b) *Under My Skin*

10. a) Golfer Ben Hogan was played by Glenn Ford in *Follow the Sun* (1951) b) Swimmer Annette Kellerman was played by Esther Williams in *Million Dollar Mermaid* (1952) c) Baseball star Grover Cleveland Alexander was played by Ronald Reagan in *The Winning Team* (1952).
11. b) Karl Malden
12. Greta Garbo was a ski instructor in *Two-Faced Woman* (1941), Marlon Brando in *The Young Lions* (1958).
13. Joe Bonaparte was played by William Holden in *Golden Boy* (1939). Danny Kenny was played by James Cagney in *City For Conquest* (1940). Paul Callan was played by Tony Curtis in *Flesh and Fury* (1952).
14. *Damn Yankees* (1958)
15. a) Mickey Shaughnessy
16. Ronald Reagan
17. a) Stacy Keach. b) John Garfield. c) Robert Ryan.
18. a) *Hatari!* (1962). b) *The Roots of Heaven* (1958). c) *Harry Black and the Tiger* (1958).
19. Babe Ruth played himself.
20. *The Stratton Story* (1949), about Monty Stratton

PAUSE FOR A MUSICAL NUMBER

(page 53)

"Oh, Give Me Time for Tenderness"	*Dark Victory*
"Rock Around the Clock"	*The Blackboard Jungle*
"Moon River"	*Breakfast at Tiffany's*
"See What the Boys in the Back Room Will Have"	*Destry Rides Again*
"Illusions"	*A Foreign Affair*
"The Sounds of Silence"	*The Graduate*
"The Sweetheart Tree"	*The Great Race*
"I'll Get By"	*A Guy Named Joe*
"High Hopes"	*A Hole in the Head*
"Moon of Manakoora"	*The Hurricane*
"Cosi-Cosa"	*A Night at the Opera*
"It Can't Be Wrong"	*Now, Voyager*
"Mam'selle"	*The Razor's Edge*
"The Shadow of Your Smile"	*The Sandpiper*
"As Long As I Live"	*Saratoga Trunk*
"The Laziest Gal in Town"	*Stage Fright*
"I'm Writing a Letter to Daddy"	*What Ever Happened to Baby Jane?*
"You're Gonna Hear From Me"	*Inside Daisy Clover*
"Long After Tonight"	*Arch of Triumph*
"Put the Blame on Mame"	*Gilda*

Bonus Photo Question: "Que Sera, Sera"

ONE GOOD MOVIE (SOMETIMES) DESERVES ANOTHER

(page 54)

1. a) Madeleine Carroll b) Dorothy Lamour c) Hedy Lamarr
2. b) *A Family Affair*
3. Joan Bennett
4. c) Van Johnson
5. a) *Nevada Smith* (1966)
6. True
7. Priscilla, Rosemary, and Lola Lane, and Gale Page
8. c) *Belles On Their Toes* (1952)
9. *Mr. Belvedere Rings the Bell* (1951)
10. b) *Dr. No* (1963)
11. Steve Reeves
12. a) Joan Caulfield b) Joan Caulfield c) Mona Freeman
13. Harry Davenport and Lucile Watson
14. b) *By the Light of the Silvery Moon* (1953)
15. a) *The Organization* (1971)
16. c) Robert Walker, Jr.
17. *Henry Aldrich, Detective*
18. a) Joel McCrea in *Internes Can't Take Money* (1937)
19. Cary Grant did not appear in either sequel. In *Topper Takes a Trip*, he was seen only in "recap" footage from the original movie.
20. Marguerite Chapman

Bonus Photo Question: b) Virginia Bruce

A CROSSWORD PUZZLE FOR MOVIE BUFFS

(page 62)

■	[1]C	[2]O	[3]I	[4]N	[5]S	[6]I	[7]N	■	[8]S	[9]T	[10]A	[11]R
[12]L	A	N	S	B	U	R	Y	■	[13]T	H	E	A
[14]O	S	A	■	■	[15]P	I	A	■	[16]S	I	R	K
[17]O	H	N	[18]O	[19]S	■	[20]S	D	[21]S	■	[22]R	Y	E
■	■	■	[23]R	T	[24]E	■	[25]S	A	[26]N	D	■	■
[27]S	[28]A	[29]B	B	A	T	[30]H	■	[31]L	O	M	[32]A	[33]S
[34]A	L	I	■	■	[35]H	U	[36]D	■	■	[37]A	D	O
[38]M	A	G	[39]D	[40]A	■	[41]K	R	[42]A	[43]S	N	A	S
■	■	[44]K	O	N	[45]G	■	[46]U	P	A	■	■	■
[47]R	[48]A	N	■	[49]N	O	[50]R	■	[51]T	O	[52]A	[53]S	[54]T
[55]O	B	I	[56]S	■	[57]I	O	[58]U	■	■	[59]G	A	R
[60]N	E	F	F	■	[61]N	A	N	[62]G	[63]R	E	Y	S
[64]A	L	E	C	■	[65]G	R	E	E	N	E	S	■

THE NAME GAME

(page 72)

1. Jane Powell
2. Dane Clark
3. Kathryn Grayson
4. Sylvia Sidney
5. Jack Benny
6. June Allyson
7. Sterling Hayden

8. Tab Hunter
9. Barry Fitzgerald
10. Yvonne DeCarlo
11. Lauren Bacall
12. Ricardo Cortez
13. Jeff Chandler
14. Paulette Goddard
15. Carole Lombard
16. Betty Hutton
17. Marie Dressler
18. Roy Rogers
19. Jean Harlow
20. Natalie Wood
21. Sandra Dee
22. Nancy Carroll
23. Martha Raye
24. Joan Crawford
25. Rita Moreno

FROM THE PAGES OF HISTORY

(page 73)

1. Jose Ferrer. a) *Deep In My Heart* (1954) b) *I Accuse* (1958) c) *Moulin Rouge* (1953)
2. Robert Morley. a) *Marie Antoinette* (1938) b) *Gilbert and Sullivan* (1953) c) *Beau Brummell* (1954)
3. Betty Hutton. a) *Incendiary Blonde* (1945) b) *The Perils of Pauline* (1947) c) *Somebody Loves Me* (1952)
4. Charlton Heston. a) *The President's Lady* (1953) b) *The Greatest Story Ever Told* (1965) c) *Khartoum* (1966)
5. Fredric March. a) *The Barretts of Wimpole Street* (1934) b) *The Adventures of Mark Twain* (1944) c) *Christopher Columbus* (1949)
6. Tony Curtis. a) *The Great Impostor* (1961) b) *The Outsider* (1962) c) *The Boston Strangler* (1968)
7. Errol Flynn. a) *Gentleman Jim* (1942) b) *Too Much, Too Soon* (1958) c) *They Died With Their Boots On* (1941)
8. Mickey Rooney. a) *Young Tom Edison* (1940) b) *Words and Music* (1948) c) *Baby Face Nelson* (1957)
9. Susan Hayward. a) *With a Song In My Heart* (1952) b) *The President's Lady* (1953) c) *I'll Cry Tomorrow* (1956)
10. Richard Burton. a) *Prince of Players* (1955) b) *Becket* (1964) c) *Anne of the Thousand Days* (1971)
11. Myrna Loy. a) *The Great Ziegfeld* (1936) b) *Parnell* (1937) c) *Cheaper By the Dozen* (1950) and *Belles On Their Toes* (1952)
12. Orson Welles. a) *Compulsion* (1959) b) *Lafayette* (1962) c) *A Man For All Seasons* (1966)
13. Claude Rains. a) *Juarez* (1939) b) *Hearts Divided* (1936) c) *Lady With Red Hair* (1940)
14. Walter Pidgeon. a) *Madame Curie* (1943) b) *Deep In My Heart* (1954) c) *Funny Girl* (1968)
15. Jason Robards, Jr. a) *Act One* (1963) b) *Al Capone* (1967) c) *Hour of the Gun* (1967)
16. Alec Guinness. a) *The Mudlark* (1950) b) *Cromwell* (1969) c) *The Last Ten Days* (1973)
17. James Mason. a) *Madame Bovary* (1949) b) *The Desert Fox* (1951) and *The Desert Rats* (1953) c) *Mayerling* (1969)
18. James Cagney. a) *Man of a Thousand Faces* (1957) b) *The Gallant Hours* (1960) c) *Love Me Or Leave Me* (1955)
19. Charles Laughton. a) *The Private Life of Henry VIII* (1933)
b) *Rembrandt* (1936) c) *Young Bess* (1953)
20.

a.	Davy Crockett	d)	John Wayne in *The Alamo* (1960)
b.	Sam Houston	h)	Richard Dix in *Man of Conquest* (1940)
c.	Jim Bowie	f)	Alan Ladd in *The Iron Mistress* (1952)
d.	"Buffalo Bill" Cody	c)	Joel McCrea in *Buffalo Bill* (1944)
e.	Jesse James	i)	Robert Wagner in *The True Story of Jesse James* (1956)
f.	Geronimo	a)	Chuck Connors in *Geronimo* (1962)
g.	Wyatt Earp	j)	James Stewart in *Cheyenne Autumn* (1964)
h.	Sitting Bull	g)	J. Carrol Naish in *Annie Get Your Gun* (1950)
i.	Billy the Kid	b)	Robert Taylor in *Billy the Kid* (1940)
j.	Wild Bill Hickok	e)	Gary Cooper in *The Plainsman* (1936)

Bonus Photo Question: *Mission to Moscow* (1943)

HALF-WAY UP THE LADDER

(page 74)

Photo 1: Sheila Ryan
Photo 2: Karen Morley
Photo 3: Stephanie Bachelor
Photo 4: June Travis
Photo 5: Evelyn Ankers
Photo 6: Marguerite Chapman
Photo 7: Peggy Dow
Photo 8: Olympe Bradna
Photo 9: Jane Frazee
Photo 10: Gale Page
Photo 11: Andrea King
Photo 12: Sally Forrest
Photo 13: Ella Raines
Photo 14: Evelyn Keyes
Photo 15: Phyllis Brooks
Photo 16: Marjorie Weaver
Photo 17: Janis Carter
Photo 18: Gloria Stuart

"THIS KID HAS TALENT!"

(page 89)

Alice Faye
1. b) *On the Avenue* (1937)
2. a) *That Night in Rio* (1941)
3. b) Don Ameche (six times to Payne's four and Power's three)

Bing Crosby
1. a) *Going Hollywood* (1933) b) *Mississippi* (1935) c) *Doctor Rhythm* (1938)
2. *Rhythm on the Range* (1936), *Doctor Rhythm* (1938), *Rhythm on the River* (1940), and *Star Spangled Rhythm* (1942)
3. a) *Sing, You Sinners* (1938) b) *Holiday Inn* (1942) c) *Riding High* (1950)

Judy Garland
1. a) *Girl Crazy* (1943) b) *Easter Parade* (1948) c) *A Star Is Born* (1954)
2. a) *The Pirate* (1948) b) *A Star Is Born* (1954) c) *In the Good Old Summertime* (1949) (originally *The Shop Around the Corner*, 1940)
3. a) *Babes in Arms* (1939).

Fred Astaire
1. a) *Roberta* (1935) b) *Swing Time* (1936) c) *Carefree* (1938)
2. a) Joan Leslie, *The Sky's the Limit* (1943) b) Vera-Ellen, *Three Little Words* (1950) c) Audrey Hepburn, *Funny Face* (1957)
3. "Let's Face the Music and Dance," in *Follow the Fleet* (1936) b) "This Heart of Mine," in *Ziegfeld Follies* (1946) c) "Girl Hunt Ballet," in *The Band Wagon* (1953).

Betty Grable
1. c) *Billy Rose's Diamond Horseshoe* (1945)
2. b) *Wabash Avenue* (1950)
3. a) *The Farmer Takes a Wife* (1953) b) *Three for the Show* (1955), earlier *Too Many Husbands* (1940) c) *When My Baby Smiles at Me* (1948), earlier *Swing High, Swing Low* (1937), both based on *Burlesque*

Gene Kelly
1. a) *Thousands Cheer* (1943) b) *Summer Stock* (1950) c) *Anchors Aweigh* (1945)
2. a) Cyd Charisse in *Brigadoon* (1954) b) Donald O'Connor in *Singin' in the Rain* (1952) c) Kay Kendall in *Les Girls* (1957)
3. b) "Love Walked In"

Jeanette MacDonald
1. *Love Me Tonight* (1932)
2. a) *Rose Marie* (1936) b) *The Girl of the Golden West* (1938) c) *Sweethearts* (1938)
3. Robert Taylor

Dan Dailey
1. a) *Mother Wore Tights* (1947) b) *My Blue Heaven* (1950) c) *When My Baby Smiles At Me* (1948)
2. *It's Always Fair Weather* (1955)
3. *There's No Business Like Show Business* (1954)

TOGETHER AGAIN FOR THE FIRST TIME
(page 90)

1. Humphrey Bogart in *The Desperate Hours* (1955). June Allyson in *The Glenn Miller Story* (1954). They co-starred in *Battle Circus* (1953).
2. Clark Gable in *Boom Town* (1940). Doris Day in *I'll See You In My Dreams* (1951). They co-starred in *Teacher's Pet* (1958).
3. John Garfield in *Humoresque* (1946). Lana Turner in *Peyton Place* (1957). They co-starred in *The Postman Always Rings Twice* (1946).
4. Bette Davis in *Watch on the Rhine* (1943). Robert Montgomery in *Night Must Fall* (1937). They co-starred in *June Bride* (1948).
5. Spencer Tracy in *Inherit the Wind* (1960). Marlene Dietrich in *Stage Fright* (1950). They co-starred in *Judgment at Nuremberg* (1961).

6. Gary Cooper in *The Friendly Persuasion* (1956). Rita Hayworth in *Pal Joey* (1957). They co-starred in *They Came to Cordura* (1959).
7. Fred Astaire in *Top Hat* (1935). Joan Leslie in *Sergeant York* (1941). They co-starred in *The Sky's the Limit* (1943).
8. Ronald Colman in *A Double Life* (1948). Ginger Rogers in *Tom, Dick and Harry* (1941). They co-starred in *Lucky Partners* (1940).
9. Wallace Beery in *Dinner At Eight* (1933). Jane Powell in *Seven Brides for Seven Brothers* (1954). They co-starred in *A Date With Judy* (1948).
10. Charles Boyer in *Gaslight* (1944). Katharine Hepburn in *State of the Union* (1948). They co-starred in *Break of Hearts* (1935).
11. James Cagney in *Angels With Dirty Faces* (1938). Sylvia Sidney in *Fury* (1936). They co-starred in *Blood on the Sun* (1945).
12. Claudette Colbert in *It Happened One Night* (1934). John Wayne in *True Grit* (1969). They co-starred in *Without Reservations* (1946).
13. Van Heflin in *Madame Bovary* (1949). Joan Crawford in *The Women* (1939). They co-starred in *Possessed* (1947).
14. Errol Flynn in *The Charge of the Light Brigade* (1936). Barbara Stanwyck in *Double Indemnity* (1944). They co-starred in *Cry Wolf* (1947).
15. Henry Fonda in *The Ox-Bow Incident* (1943). Lauren Bacall in *To Have and Have Not* (1944). They co-starred in *Sex and the Single Girl* (1964).
16. Kirk Douglas in *Detective Story* (1951). Ava Gardner in *The Sun Also Rises*. They co-starred in *Seven Days in May* (1964).
17. Ralph Bellamy in *Rosemary's Baby* (1968). Greer Garson in *Pride and Prejudice* (1940). They co-starred in *Sunrise at Campobello* (1960).
18. Rex Harrison in *The Agony and the Ecstasy* (1965). Susan Hayward in *Valley of the Dolls* (1967). They co-starred in *The Honey Pot* (1967).
19. Laurence Olivier in *Sleuth* (1972). Jennifer Jones in *Tender is the Night* (1962). They co-starred in *Carrie* (1952).
20. Clifton Webb in *The Razor's Edge* (1946). Ginger Rogers in *Stage Door* (1937). They co-starred in *Dreamboat* (1952).
Bonus Photo Question: *Susan Lenox: Her Fall and Rise*

THE CHILDREN'S HOUR
(page 91)

1. Bonita Granville
2. Jackie Cooper
3. Claude Jarman, Jr.
4. Virginia Weidler
5. Brandon de Wilde
6. Jackie Butch Jenkins
7. Mickey Rooney
8. Shirley Temple
9. Mark Lester
10. Deanna Durbin
11. Bobby Driscoll
12. Skippy Homeier
13. Patty Duke
14. Margaret O'Brien
15. Dean Stockwell

16. Roddy McDowall
17. Patty McCormack
18. Freddie Bartholomew
19. Peggy Ann Garner
20. Karen Dotrice
Bonus Photo Question: Larry Simms

BLACK STAR
(page 92)

1. Juano Hernandez. *Intruder in the Dust* (1949)
2. Claudia McNeil. *A Raisin in the Sun* (1961)
3. Louise Beavers. *Imitation of Life* (1934)
4. Godfrey Cambridge. *Cotton Comes to Harlem* (1970). Also *Come Back, Charleston Blue* (1972).
5. Sidney Poitier. *Lilies of the Field* (1963)
6. Paul Winfield. *Sounder* (1972)
7. Butterfly McQueen. *Gone With the Wind* (1939)
8. Sidney Poitier. *To Sir, With Love* (1967)
9. Ethel Waters. *The Member of the Wedding* (1952)
10. James Earl Jones. *The Great White Hope* (1970)
11. Brock Peters. *To Kill a Mockingbird* (1962)
12. Eddie Anderson. *The Green Pastures* (1936)
13. Paul Robeson. *The Emperor Jones* (1933)
14. Paul Robeson in *Show Boat* (1936) William Warfield in *Show Boat* (1951)
15. Ethel Waters. *Cabin in the Sky* (1943)
Bonus Photo Question: Hattie McDaniel

THE MOVIE DETECTIVES
(page 97)

Photos 1, 2, and 3: The detective is Philo Vance.
Photo 1:   William Powell
Photo 2:   Warren William
Photo 3:   Paul Lukas
Photo 4:   The attorney is Perry Mason. The actor is Warren William.
Photo 5:   The detective is Dick Tracy, here in *Dick Tracy's G-Men*. The actor is Ralph Byrd.
Photo 6:   Boston Blackie, played by Chester Morris
Photo 7:   Torchy Blane
Photo 8:   The detective is Ellery Queen. The actor is Ralph Bellamy.
Photo 9:   "The Crime Doctor," played by Warner Baxter
Photo 10: The actor is George Sanders. The detective is Simon Templar, known as "The Saint." (The scene shown is from *The Saint's Double Trouble* in 1940.)
Photo 11: Tom Conway
Photo 12: Bonita Granville
Photo 13: *The Adventures of Sherlock Holmes* (1939)

THE MEN AT THE HELM
(page 114)

I.   Otto Preminger
A. *Centennial Summer* (1946)
B. *Whirlpool* (1950)

C. False. He directed Jean Seberg in *Bonjour Tristesse* (1959).
D. Dorothy Dandridge
E. *Seven Days in May*
II. Vincente Minnelli
A. Lucille Bremer and Fred Astaire
B. *The Bad and the Beautiful* (1952). Lana Turner
C. False. George Stevens won for *A Place in the Sun. An American in Paris* won the Best Picture award.
D. *Designing Woman* (1957)
E. *Please Don't Eat the Daisies*
III. William Wellman
A. *The Public Enemy*
B. *The Great Man's Lady* (1942). *Lady of Burlesque* (1943)
C. *The Ox-Bow Incident* (1943)
D. George Murphy, James Whitmore, Richard Jaeckel
E. *Blood Alley* (1955)
IV. Billy Wilder
A. False. Wilder was nominated but did not win for *Sunset Boulevard*.
B. *Stalag 17* (1953). *Sabrina* (1954)
C. *Double Indemnity* (1944)
D. *Avanti!* (1972)
E. *Love in the Afternoon* (1957)
V.   Mervyn LeRoy
A. *Gold Diggers of 1933*
B. Van Heflin for *Johnny Eager*
C. *Little Women* (George Cukor) and *In the Good Old Summertime*, a remake of Ernst Lubitsch's *The Shop Around the Corner*
D. *Teahouse of the August Moon*
E. *The Devil At Four O'Clock*

MOVIE PEOPLE
(page 116)

Hermes Pan ..... Dance director, associated with Fred Astaire in the thirties
Yakima Canutt .... Handled stunts for many films
Max Fleischer .... Animator, created Popeye, Betty Boop
Travis Banton .... Costume designer for Mae West in the thirties
Harry Cohn .... Powerful head of Columbia Pictures for many years
Dorothy Arzner ...Director of *Christopher Strong, Craig's Wife*
Marni Nixon ..Singer who has dubbed the voices of many stars
Dudley Nichols .... Screenwriter, wrote *The Informer, Stagecoach*, etc.
Stanley Donen .... Director of *On the Town, Funny Face, Lucky Lady*, etc.
James Wong Howe ....Cinematographer, *Kings Row, The Rose Tattoo*, etc.
Cedric Gibbons .... MGM's Art Director for many years
Dimitri Tiomkin ....Composer, won Academy Award for *High Noon*
Frances Marion .... Long-time screenwriter: *The Champ, Dinner at Eight*, etc.
Busby Berkeley .... Song-and-dance director, noted for kaleidoscopic effects
Cecil Beaton ....Designer for *Gigi* and *My Fair Lady*
Julius J. Epstein ....Screenwriter: *Four Daughters, My Foolish Heart*, etc.

Rouben Mamoulian . . . . Director of 1932 version of *Dr. Jekyll and Mr. Hyde*
Edith Head . . . . Award-winning designer: *The Heiress, Samson and Delilah*, etc.
Dalton Trumbo . . . . Screenwriter, one of the "Hollywood Ten"
Natalie Kalmus . . . Advisor on all Technicolor films, 1933-1963
Merian C. Cooper . . . . Producer associated with *King Kong* (original version)

Erich Wolfgang Korngold . . . . Composer, won Academy Award for *The Adventures of Robin Hood*
Tod Browning . . . . Director of *Dracula* and *Freaks*
Dudley Nichols . . . . Screenwriter: wrote *The Informer, Stagecoach*, etc.
Will Hays . . . . . Author of the screen's Production Code in 1930

THE MOVIE SONGSMITHS (TWO)
(page 131)

"Easy to Love"	Cole Porter	*Born to Dance*
"By Strauss"	George Gershwin	*An American in Paris*
"My One and Only Highland Fling"	Harry Warren	*The Barkleys of Broadway*
"Now It Can Be Told"	Irving Berlin	*Alexander's Ragtime Band*
"Never Gonna Dance"	Jerome Kern	*Swing Time*
"It's a New World"	Harold Arlen	*A Star is Born*
"All I Owe Ioway"	Richard Rodgers	*State Fair*
"Small World"	Jule Styne	*Gypsy*
"Sunday, Monday, or Always"	Jimmy Van Heusen	*Dixie*
"You Are My Lucky Star"	Nacio Herb Brown	*Broadway Melody of 1936*
"Love In Bloom"	Ralph Rainger	*She Loves Me Not*
"They're Either Too Young or Too Old"	Arthur Schwartz	*Thank Your Lucky Stars*
"Orchids in the Moonlight"	Vincent Youmans	*Flying Down to Rio*
"The Night They Invented Champagne"	Frederick Loewe	*Gigi*
"Thinking Of You"	Bert Kalmar	*Three Little Words*

THE MASTER OF MENACE
(page 137)

1. a) *Rope* (1948). b) *Vertigo* (1958). c) *The Man Who Knew Too Much* (1956). All three roles were played by James Stewart.
2. a) *The Lady Vanishes* (1938). b) *Strangers on a Train* (1951). c) *Foreign Correspondent* (1940).
3. a) *A Woman Alone* (British title: *Sabotage*) (1936). b) *Frenzy* (1972). c) *Dial M For Murder* (1954).
4. a) They are grappling. He is trying to throw her off the train but falls off himself. The film is *Shadow of a Doubt* (1943). b) A body is inside the chest—the victim of a senseless murder by Brandon and Philip. The film is *Rope* (1948). c) This was the first sign that the community of the birds was turning inexplicably vicious. The film is *The Birds* (1963).
5. Raymond Massey. Ray Milland appeared in *Dial M For Murder* (1954). James Mason appeared in *North by Northwest* (1959). Sean Connery appeared in *Marnie* (1964).
6. *Torn Curtain* (1966)
7. *Notorious* (1946)
8. a) Alastair Sim. b) Jessie Royce Landis. c) Patricia Collinge

9. a) Joan Fontaine in *Suspicion* (1941). b) Grace Kelly in *To Catch a Thief* (1955). c) Eva Marie Saint in *North By Northwest* (1959)
10. Harry's dead, and the cast principals are trying to find a way to dispose of his body.
11. Granger's partners-in-crime were played by John Dall in *Rope*, and by Robert Walker in *Strangers on a Train*.
12. *Topaz*
13. c) a man wrongly accused of theft
14. a) Maureen O'Hara. b) Shirley MacLaine. c) Tippi Hedren
15. Martin Balsam
16. c) Leslie Banks
17. a) *The Paradine Case* (1947). b) *The Birds* (1963). c) *Notorious* (1946)
18. *The Thirty-Nine Steps* (1935)
19. *Rebecca* (1940)
20. *Under Capricorn* (1949)
Bonus Photo Question: *Mr. and Mrs. Smith*

ABOUT THE CONTRIBUTORS

Jeanine Basinger is an Associate Professor of Film at Wesleyan University in Middletown, Connecticut, where she teaches courses on all aspects of American film history and aesthetics. She is the author of three books in the Pyramid Illustrated History of the Movies: *Shirley Temple*, *Gene Kelly*, and *Lana Turner*. In addition, her articles have appeared in numerous publications, including *The New York Times* and *American Film*, and in several anthologies, including the first *Movie Buff's Book*.

Curtis F. Brown is the author of *Star-Spangled Kitsch* and of two books in the Pyramid film series on Ingrid Bergman and Jean Harlow. He also contributed to the first *Movie Buff's Book*. A film addict for many years, he is an administrative assistant at a New York college.

Foster Hirsch is the author of *Elizabeth Taylor* and *Edward G. Robinson* in the Pyramid film series. Assistant Professor of English and Film at Brooklyn College, he has also written books on the epic film and on George Kelly, Tennessee Williams, and Laurence Olivier. He has contributed articles to numerous publications, including the first *Movie Buff's Book*.

Judith M. Kass is the author of *Olivia de Havilland* and a forthcoming book on Ava Gardner in the Pyramid Illustrated History of the Movies, and of a study of Don Siegel in *The Hollywood Professionals*, vol. 4. She has written film criticism for *The Soho Weekly News* and writes and edits the United Artists/16 newsletter, *Images*. Ms. Kass has been the film program coordinator for The New York Cultural Center and is a graduate of the State University of New York.

Patrick McGilligan is the author of a book on Ginger Rogers in the Pyramid series, and has also written *Cagney: The Actor as Auteur*. He is presently working on a novel, and at least a hundred other mysterious projects.

Leonard Maltin is perhaps best-known for his book *TV Movies*, a guide to 10,000 films on television. He has written many other books on film, and also organized the Museum of Modern Art's Bicentennial salute to American film comedy. He teaches at the New School for Social Research in New York City.

Lee Edward Stern, author of *The Movie Musical* in the Pyramid film series, is a public relations executive, writer, and radio commentator. When he was a young actor in summer and winter stock productions, he became convinced that the villains always get the best lines.

Tony Thomas has written more than a dozen books on the history of Hollywood and its personalities, including accounts of the careers of Errol Flynn, Marlon Brando, Gene Kelly, and Busby Berkeley. His books on Burt Lancaster and Gregory Peck are part of the Pyramid film series. Long a producer with the Canadian Broadcasting Corporation, he has specialized in studying film music and has produced many record albums of soundtrack material.

Jerry Vermilye is the author of *Bette Davis*, *Cary Grant*, *Barbara Stanwyck*, and a forthcoming book on Ida Lupino, in the Pyramid film series. He has also written *The Films of Elizabeth Taylor*. The movie-listings editor of *TV Guide*, he has contributed articles to leading film magazines, and to the first *Movie Buff's Book*.

James Winchester was a staff writer for the biweekly trade magazine for exhibitors, *The Independent Film Journal*. He also worked in the publicity department of American International Pictures.

ABOUT THE EDITOR

Ted Sennett is the author of *Warner Brothers Presents*, a tribute to the great Warners' films of the thirties and forties, and of *Lunatics and Lovers*, on the long-vanished but well-remembered "screwball" movie comedies of the past. He is the General Editor of the Pyramid Illustrated History of the Movies, and edited the first *Movie Buff's Book*. He recently edited *The Old-Time Radio Book*, a collection of articles, quizzes, and photographs on the golden years of radio, and he is presently writing a book on the famous television program, "Your Show of Shows." He is Editor-in-Chief of *Bijou: The Magazine of the Movies*.